Editor

Eric Migliaccio

Editorial Project Manager

Ina Massler Levin, M.A.

Editor-in-Chief

Sharon Coan, M.S. Ed.

Cover Artist

Denise Bauer

Art Coordinator

Kevin Barnes

Imaging

Alfred Lau

Product Manager

Phil Garcia

Publisher

Mary D. Smith, M.S. Ed.

Take Five Minutes:
American History Class Openers

Reflective and Critical

Challeng...

Author

D. Antonio Cantu, Ph.D.

Teacher Created Resources, Inc.

6421 Industry Way

Westminster, CA 92683

www.teachercreated.com

ISBN-0-7439-3641-8

©2002 Teacher Created Resources, Inc.

Reprinted, 2005

Made in U.S.A.

Table of Contents

Table of Contents *(cont.)*

Reflective and Critical-Thinking Activities *(cont.)*

Appendix

Introduction

The first five minutes of a class are among the most critical in teaching for the role they play in setting the instructional stage and transitioning students into the lesson. *Take Five Minutes: Reflective and Critical Thinking American History Class Openers* is designed to assist teachers in this task through the integration of a variety of engaging activities that not only set the stage for American history lessons but also provoke higher order thinking.

This book includes themes addressing topics from American history that span from the pre-Columbian era to the present. Each of the 72 themes includes six different types of reflective and critical thinking activities: journal writing prompts, time lines, decision-making scenarios, concept maps, Venn diagrams, and vee heuristics. (An overview of each of these activities can be found on pages 5–11.) A total of 17 activities from these six categories are included for each theme, providing students with over 1,200 opportunities to reflect upon and critically examine the major individuals, events, movements, and issues that are key to our understanding of American history.

The activities contained within *Take Five Minutes: Reflective and Critical Thinking American History Class Openers* may be used in the following manner:

- Teachers may choose to reproduce the pages containing the activities for each individual theme and distribute them to students, write them on the chalkboard/dry-erase board, or display them on a transparency or PowerPoint slide.

- Students then have the opportunity to immediately begin engaging in their daily reflective and critical thinking activity. When completed, teachers may have students turn in their work, maintain it in their student portfolio, and/or use student responses as the focus of a classroom discussion.

- Students may use their notebooks or one of the activity sheet handouts included in the book (of which two versions are provided for each of the six types of activities) to record their response to the question or task for that particular day.

- Teachers may choose to use the charts included in the book to monitor individual student progress, class progress, or as a lesson planning aid to assist in the selection of activities for each class period.

- This book is intentionally designed to give teachers the opportunity to integrate any number of these activities for each theme into their classroom curriculum. Teachers may choose to integrate only one or two of these activities if time is limited, or they can easily add more to fit their neeeds if time allows. In addition, teachers may elect to use these activities as pre-assessment devices to determine what students already know about a specific theme or topic in American history. Teachers may also assign the activities as homework, in preparation for classroom discussion the next day, or as an independent learning activity to be completed in class at the conclusion of a daily lesson. Finally, teachers may find these activities serve as ideal unit review questions or even as assessment items on a unit quiz or test.

The following pages (pages 5–11) contain brief summaries and completed samples of the six different types of activities included in *Take Five Minutes: Reflective and Critical Thinking American History Class Openers.*

Introduction (cont.)

Activities Overview

Journal Prompts

Three journal questions are included for each of the 72 themes. These questions serve as ideal prompts or vehicles for engaging students in all levels of thinking, from the knowledge level to the evaluation level. Teachers may choose to use the full-page activity handout sheet included at the back of the book (page 158)—which allows students to delve further into a topic in order to demonstrate a deeper understanding—or the other activity sheet version (page 159) with all three journal response sections on one page—which allows for more concise responses while still serving to monitor student comprehension.

Sample Journal Prompt

Prompt: "The role of Christopher Columbus in history is greatly debated. Is his legacy positive, negative, or both? Explain."

I think that Columbus should be remembered in history both for the good and bad that came about as a result of his voyage in 1492. His discovery of a new sea route to the new world resulted in a number of good or positive things such as the increase in trade between Europe and North and South America. Also, it led to the founding of settlements by the Spanish, and later, the English, such as St. Augustine and Jamestown. Who knows, maybe the United States would never have been created if not for Columbus. While there are good things that happened as a result of Christopher Columbus' voyage, there were also a number of bad things. First, the conquistadors did not treat the native people with respect and often did terrible things to them such as working them as slaves and killing them in battle. Many of the native people also died as a result of the diseases that the Spanish brought over with them. Another bad thing that resulted from Columbus' "discovery" of America was the slave trade that developed between Africa and the New World, which would last for centuries. Overall, I think that you can't say Columbus should be remembered in history as simply a positive or negative person, instead he should be remembered as a person whose accomplishments brought about both good and bad things for the people of the world.

Introduction (cont.)

Activities Overview (cont.)

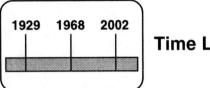

Time Lines

Each of the themes includes three different historical topics students can use as a focus for the construction of historical time lines. Students can use their textbooks, class notes, and other resources to assist in the design of each time line. Time-line activities are ideal for gauging student understanding of historical perspective and casual relationships. There are two different time-line handout versions included at the back of the book. The first (page 160) allows students to list a greater number of events for a given topic, as well as provide a more detailed description of each event. The other time-line handout (page 161) provides for all three topics included in each theme to be completed on a single page, allowing students to visually compare and contrast the events for each topic.

Sample Time Line

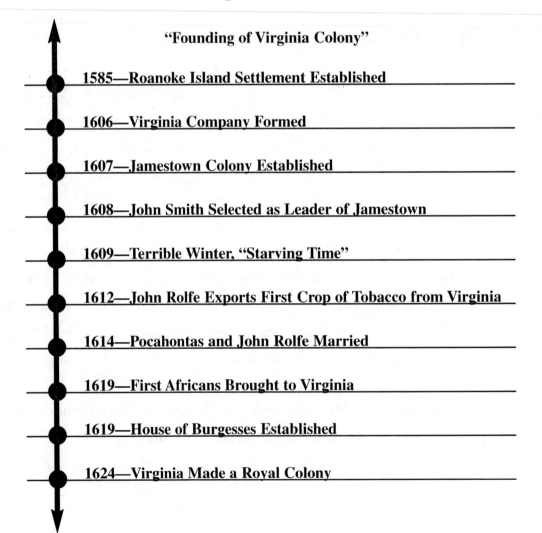

"Founding of Virginia Colony"

1585—Roanoke Island Settlement Established

1606—Virginia Company Formed

1607—Jamestown Colony Established

1608—John Smith Selected as Leader of Jamestown

1609—Terrible Winter, "Starving Time"

1612—John Rolfe Exports First Crop of Tobacco from Virginia

1614—Pocahontas and John Rolfe Married

1619—First Africans Brought to Virginia

1619—House of Burgesses Established

1624—Virginia Made a Royal Colony

Introduction *(cont.)*

Activities Overview *(cont.)*

 **Decision-Making Scenarios**

There are three decision-making scenarios provided for each theme. These scenarios allow students to demonstrate both convergent and divergent thinking skills. They also provide a way for students to participate in activities that introduce historical empathy as an instructional means for building student understanding. Teachers may elect to use either the full-page journal or notebook handout (page 162) for students to respond to these decision-making questions, or the modified version, which includes space for students to respond to all three questions for each theme on one page (page 163). In addition, there is a full-page decision-making chart (page 164) included for those teachers who desire a more structured student response to these questions.

Sample Decision-Making Scenario

> **Scenario: "If you were an abolitionist, would you have commended or condemned John Brown for his 1856 attack on the pro-slavery town of Pottawatomie Creek, Kansas, which resulted in the death of five settlers? Explain."**
>
> I think if I was around in the 1850s, I would have worked hard to help bring about an end to slavery just as Frederick Douglass, Harriet Beecher Stowe, and many others did. I might have even traveled to Kansas during the debate over slavery and have worked to make sure Kansas entered the Union as a free state. The problem I have is not with what John Brown was fighting for but in the way he went about doing it. While I know that some abolitionists might have been happy when they heard the news about what happened at Pottawatomie Creek, I think many of them probably would have reacted the same way I feel, and that is it is never right for people to kill other people in cold blood just because of something they believe in. Slavery is wrong, but so is killing people, and two wrongs don't make a right. I think if I was around at this time, I would have written a letter to my local newspaper or attended an abolitionist's meeting so I could tell them how I felt. I could support a number of things the abolitionists did back then, such as writing books like *Uncle Tom's Cabin* or working on the Underground Railroad—I even would have fought in the Civil War—but I don't believe I could have supported or participated in the kind of things John Brown and his followers did at Pottawatomie Creek. The end doesn't always justify the means.

Introduction (cont.)

Activities Overview (cont.)

Decision-Making Scenarios (cont.)

Below is a sample of a full-page decision-making chart, which has been included for those teachers who desire a more structured student response to these questions.

Sample Decision-Making Scenario (Chart Format)

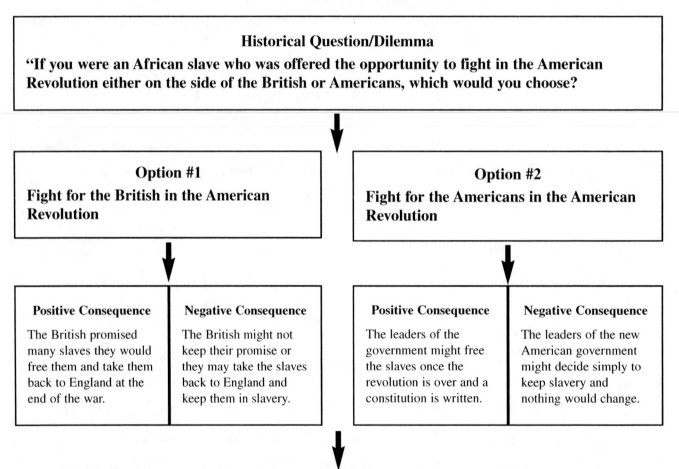

Historical Question/Dilemma

"If you were an African slave who was offered the opportunity to fight in the American Revolution either on the side of the British or Americans, which would you choose?

Option #1
Fight for the British in the American Revolution

Option #2
Fight for the Americans in the American Revolution

Positive Consequence

The British promised many slaves they would free them and take them back to England at the end of the war.

Negative Consequence

The British might not keep their promise or they may take the slaves back to England and keep them in slavery.

Positive Consequence

The leaders of the government might free the slaves once the revolution is over and a constitution is written.

Negative Consequence

The leaders of the new American government might decide simply to keep slavery and nothing would change.

Decision

If I was an African slave during the American Revolution, I think I would fight for the American side for two reasons. First, I think the British would not keep their promise and would possibly take me and my family back to England to serve as slaves. Second, I hear the American political and military leaders talk a lot about freedom and liberty, and if they truly believe in these things, they will have to free the slaves once the war is over and after a new constitution is passed and the government is established.

Introduction (cont.)

Activities Overview (cont.)

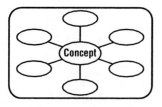

Concept Maps

A total of four key concepts—which include issues, movements, innovations, theories, and other events from American history—are included for each theme. These items serve as ideal vehicles for engaging students in concept mapping or pattern noting activities, designed to help teachers determine the breadth and depth of student knowledge and understanding. Teachers should have students write the listed concept in the center circle on the map and then expand on the concept using one- or two-word phrases to describe related characteristics (individuals, events, consequences, etc.). Students can either design a semantic concept map, placing these related characteristics in the appropriate location (circle or box); or teachers can ask students to design a structured overview concept map that also includes the listing of the verb on the stem or line that connects these items. The book includes a full-page version of a concept map (page 165) that allows for both structured overview and semantic concept mapping. There is also another version provided (pages 166 and 167) that includes two concept maps per page.

Sample Concept Map

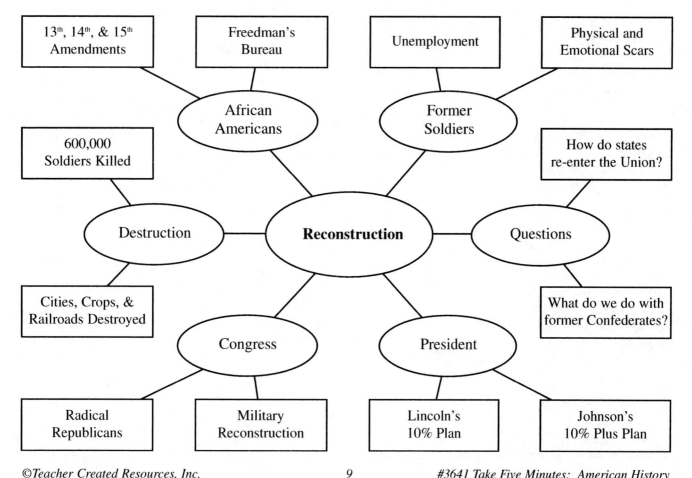

Introduction *(cont.)*

Activities Overview *(cont.)*

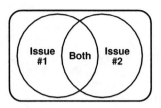 **Venn Diagrams**

Each theme contains two questions designed for students to respond through the use of a Venn diagram. These questions, as well as the resulting Venn diagram, are great vehicles for engaging students in analytical and convergent thinking. Teachers can instruct students in both the number of differences and similarities that should be included in their response, as well as whether students should simply list or list and describe each of these items. A full-page handout of a Venn diagram is provided at the back of the book (page 168), as well as a version that includes both Venn diagrams for each theme listed on a single page (page 169).

Sample Venn Diagram

"Compare and contrast the events that led America to break from their official policy of neutrality and enter World War I and World War II.

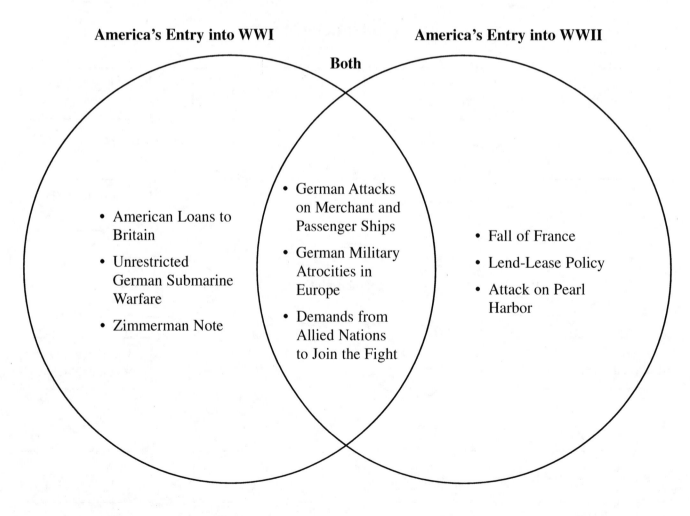

America's Entry into WWI

America's Entry into WWII

Both

- American Loans to Britain
- Unrestricted German Submarine Warfare
- Zimmerman Note

- German Attacks on Merchant and Passenger Ships
- German Military Atrocities in Europe
- Demands from Allied Nations to Join the Fight

- Fall of France
- Lend-Lease Policy
- Attack on Pearl Harbor

Introduction *(cont.)*

Activities Overview *(cont.)*

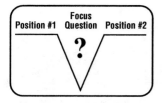

Vee Heuristics

Two focus questions are provided for each of the 72 themes that allow students to respond through the use of a vee heuristic. With a somewhat similar format to that of a Venn diagram, a vee heuristic is designed for students to analyze dichotomous positions, policies, theories, decisions, movements, innovations, and events in American history. The vee heuristic encourages students to delve further into the dichotomous positions addressed in the focus question, because there is no provision for a comparison as there would be in a Venn diagram activity. The focus question should be listed in the center of the vee heuristic, with the two dichotomous positions labeled to the left and right of the question. A handout containing a full-page vee heuristic is provided on page 170, as well as a version that includes both of the vee heuristics for each theme on one page (page 171).

Sample Vee Heuristic

1. 1960s Civil Rights Movement

2. 1950s Civil Rights Movement

How did the tactics, successes, and setbacks of the 1960s Civil Rights Movement differ from those of the previous decade?

- 1960—Greensboro Sit-In movement starts

- 1961—Freedom Rides begin

- 1962—James Meredith attempts to attend the University of Mississippi

- 1963—Martin Luther King, Jr., march on Washington

- 1963—Malcolm X enters as another leader in the civil rights movement

- 1964—Civil Right Act and 1965 Voting Rights Act passed

- 1968—Martin Luther King, Jr., assassinated in Memphis

- Korean War = 1st desegregated military

- 1954—*Brown vs. Board of Education* court decision

- 1955—Rosa Parks refuses to give up bus seat

- 1955—Montgomery bus boycott

- 1955—Martin Luther King, Jr., becomes leader of the civil rights movement

- 1957—Crisis at Little Rock Central High School

- 1957—Civil Rights Act passed

Introduction *(cont.)*

National Standards Connection

The teaching activities included in this book engage students in the following standards:

National Standards for History[1]

Historical Thinking Skills	Journal Writing	Time Line	Decision Making	Concept Map	Venn Diagram	Vee Heuristic
Chronological Thinking	X	X		X		
Historical Comprehension	X		X		X	X
Historical Analysis and Interpretation	X	X	X	X	X	X
Historical Research Capabilities		X		X		
Historical Issues Analysis and Decision-Making	X		X	X	X	X

National Council for History Education[2]

Habit of the Mind	Journal Writing	Time Line	Decision Making	Concept Map	Venn Diagram	Vee Heuristic
Understand the significance of the past	X		X		X	X
Develop discriminating memory	X	X	X	X		
Develop historical empathy	X		X			
Acquire a comprehension of diverse cultures	X	X	X	X	X	X
Understand how things happen and change	X	X	X		X	X
Comprehend the interplay of change and continuity		X		X	X	X
Prepare to live with uncertainties	X		X			
Grasp the complexity of historical causation		X			X	X
Appreciate tentative nature of judgements about past	X		X		X	X
Recognize the importance of individuals in history	X	X	X	X		
Appreciate the force of the non-rational in history	X		X	X	X	X
Understand relationship between geography and history		X		X	X	X
Read widely and critically	X	X		X		

Introduction *(cont.)*

National Standards Connection *(cont.)*

National Council for the Social Studies Curriculum Standards[3]

Theme II—Time, Continuity, and Change	Journal Writing	Time Line	Decision Making	Concept Map	Venn Diagram	Vee Heuristic
Demonstrate historical knowledge is socially influenced	X		X		X	X
Apply key concepts such as time, chronology, causality	X	X	X	X	X	X
Identify significant historical periods & patterns of change	X	X	X			
Systematically employ process of critical historical inquiry	X		X	X	X	
Investigate and interpret multiple historical viewpoints	X	X	X	X	X	X
Apply modes of historical inquiry to analyze developments	X		X		X	X

1. National Center for History in the Schools, *National Standards for History: Basic Edition* (Los Angeles: National Center for History in the Schools, 1996).

2. Bradley Commission on History in Schools, *Building a History Curriculum: Guidelines for Teaching History in Schools* (Westlake, Ohio: National Council for History Education, 1995); Paul Gagnon and the Bradley Commission on History in Schools, eds., Historical Literacy: The Case for History in American Education (Boston: Houghton Mifflin, 1991), 25.

3. National Council for the Social Studies, *Expectations of Excellence: Curriculum Standards for Social Studies* (Washington, D.C.: National Council for Social Studies, 1994).

Native America

Journal Prompts

- What can we learn from studying American history?

- How did the first people come to settle what is today known as America?

- What attracted these first Americans to this hemisphere?

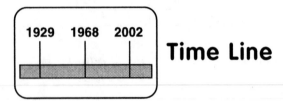

Time Line

Develop a time line listing events relevant to the following themes:

- North-American Settlements

- Mesoamerican Settlements

- South-American Settlements

Decision-Making Scenarios

- If you were one of the first inhabitants of North America, where would you settle? Explain why.

- Describe what a typical day would be like for a young Aztec living in the capital city of Tenochtitlan during the 14th century.

- What would one of your diary entries read like for a young Aztec living in the Andean highlands during the 15th century?

Native America *(cont.)*

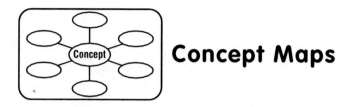 ## Concept Maps

Develop a concept map for each of the following:

- America
- History
- Indians or Native Americans
- Migration

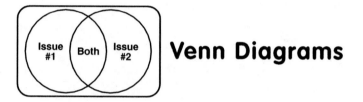 ## Venn Diagrams

Woodland Indian Cultures vs. Southwestern Indian Cultures: Compare and contrast the Native American cultures that developed in the Eastern Woodlands with those that developed in the North American Southwest.

Aztec Civilization vs. Incan Civilization: Compare and contrast 14th century Aztec civilization of Mesoamerica with the Incan civilization of South America.

 ## Vee Heuristics

Early Native American Society & Culture vs. Present-Day Society & Culture: How did early Native American society and culture differ from that of today?

Native Americans' Motivations vs. European Explorers' Motivations: What inspired Native Americans to migrate to America, and how did their motivations differ from the European explorers who would follow?

Age of Exploration

Journal Prompts

- What prompted so many Europeans to set sail for another land? Is that same sense of adventure still around today? Explain.

- If so many other explorers, such as Leif Ericson, "discovered" North America centuries before 1492, why do we give Christopher Columbus so much credit?

- The role of Christopher Columbus in history is greatly debated. Is his legacy positive, negative, or both? Explain.

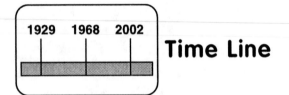

Time Line

Develop a time line listing events relevant to the following themes:

- Spanish and Portuguese Explorers and Exploration

- English and Dutch Explorers and Exploration

- French Explorers and Exploration

Decision-Making Scenarios

- If you were hired by Prince Henry the Navigator to teach Portuguese sailors during the 15th century, what navigation instruments or principles would you teach to them? Explain.

- If you were a young Spaniard approached by Columbus to go on his first voyage, would you go? Explain.

- What would your diary entry for September 6, 1522, read like if you were a member of Ferdinand Magellan's crew and had just completed your voyage around the world?

Age of Exploration *(cont.)*

 ## Concept Maps

Develop a concept map for each of the following:

- Age of Discovery
- Colonization
- Explorer or Exploration
- New World

 ## Venn Diagrams

Portuguese Explorers vs. Spanish Explorers: Compare and contrast the motivation, successes, and failures of Portuguese and Spanish explorers during the 15th and 16th centuries.

French Explorers vs. English Explorers: Compare and contrast the motivation, successes, and failures of French and English explorers during the 15th and 16th centuries.

 ## Vee Heuristics

Pre-1492 European Exploration vs. Post-1492 European Exploration: How did the focus and course of European exploration differ after 1492?

Explorers' Motivations vs. Settlers' Motivations: What inspired European explorers to chart a course for the "New World," and how did their motivation differ from families that would migrate to this hemisphere decades later?

Three Worlds Meet

Journal Prompts

- If you were a young Native American living in late 15ᵗʰ-century America, what would a typical diary entry prior to and after 1492 look like?

- How could the Spanish conquistadors have militarily conquered, in such a short period of time, such great civilizations of the Americas that had survived for centuries?

- One legacy of the Native Americans is the use of Indian terms in the names of American cities, states, rivers, etc. Is it justified, however, to use Native American names and symbols today as mascots and names of sports teams?

Time Line

Develop a time line listing events relevant to the following themes:

- Spanish Conquest of Mesoamerica and South America
- Settlement of North America
- Rise of the African Slave Trade

Decision-Making Scenarios

- If you were a Native American living in the Americas during the early 16th century, what would you have done to try to prevent Europeans from invading your land?

- What would one of your diary entries read like if you were a Spanish conquistador traveling with Hernando Cortez in Mexico during the Spanish Conquest?

- If you worked as a clerk for Bartolome de Las Casas, a Spanish priest who witnessed the terrible treatment of Native Americans at the hands of the Spanish, what would you do to help bring an end to this injustice?

Three Worlds Meet (cont.)

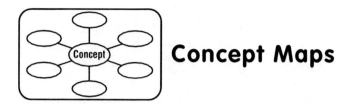 ## Concept Maps

Develop a concept map for each of the following:

- Colombian or Triangular Trade

- Conquistador

- Encomienda System

- Slavery

 ## Venn Diagrams

Treatment of Native Americans by Spanish Conquistadors vs. Treatment of Native Americans by Other European Explorers: Compare and contrast the treatment of Native Americans by the Spanish conquistadors with that of other European explorers.

Treatment of Native Americans in 1492 vs. Treatment of Native Americans Today: Compare and contrast the treatment of Native Americans in 1492 with that of today.

 ## Vee Heuristics

Native Americans Perspective vs. European Perspective: How did Europeans and Native Americans differ in their interpretation of the significance of 1492?

Native-American Beliefs & Values vs. European Beliefs & Values: How did Native-American values and beliefs differ from those of the Europeans?

Early Settlement in the Colonies

Journal Prompts

- Why do some individuals in history, such as Pocahontas, become a part of pop culture (e.g., movies, children's books, cartoons), while others are all but forgotten?

- Would racism have endured for so long in America if not for the introduction of slavery in the colonies? Explain.

- Compare and contrast society's perception of tobacco in Colonial Virginia with that of today.

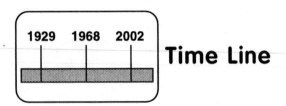

Time Line

Develop a time line listing events relevant to the following themes:

- Founding of Virginia Colony

- Founding of Plymouth Colony

- Development of Early Colonial Government and Governing Documents (e.g., Mayflower Compact)

Decision-Making Scenarios

- If you were a Jamestown resident who survived the "starving time" of the winter of 1609-10, would you return to England the next spring or remain in the Virginia colony? Explain.

- If you were a young Native American who came in contact with European settlers, would you help them out during their early period of settlement when they needed such assistance (as Squanto did) or let them suffer for trespassing on your homeland?

- If you were a young African who was taken from your family and sold into slavery in America, what would you do to survive the "middle passage" and captivity?

Early Settlement in the Colonies *(cont.)*

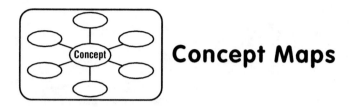

Concept Maps

Develop a concept map for each of the following:

- Freedom
- Middle Passage
- Pilgrims
- "Starving Time"

Venn Diagrams

Virginia Colony vs. Plymouth Colony: Compare and contrast the founding and settlement of the Virginia and Plymouth Colonies.

Treatment of Indentured Servants vs. Treatment of African Slaves: Compare and contrast the treatment of indentured servants and African slaves in the English Colonies.

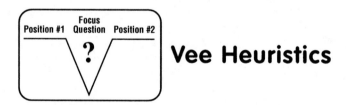

Vee Heuristics

Thanksgiving in 1621 vs. Thanksgiving Today: What are the similarities and differences between the observance/celebration of Thanksgiving in 1621 and today?

Establishment of the House of Burgesses vs. Introduction of African Labor in the Colonies: What is the historical significance and irony of the following two events (both of which occurred in the Virginia Colony in 1619): establishment of the House of Burgesses and introduction of African labor in the colonies?

Founding of the 13 Colonies

Journal Prompts

- What role should religion play in the governance of this nation?
- What role do dissenters such as Anne Hutchinson and Roger Williams play in American history? Are rebels, reformers, and dissenters celebrated more in American history than those who support the status quo? Explain.
- If you were a young Quaker living in England during the 17th century who escaped religious persecution by coming to Pennsylvania, what would you include in a letter to friends who remained?

1929   1968   2002

Time Line

Develop a time line listing events relevant to the founding of the original 13 colonies:

- Virginia
- New Hampshire
- Massachusetts
- Maryland
- Connecticut

- Rhode Island
- South Carolina
- North Carolina
- New York

- New Jersey
- Pennsylvania
- Delaware
- Georgia

Decision-Making Scenarios

- If you and your family were going to migrate to the "New World," which colony would you have chosen to reside in and why?
- If you were a resident of Massachusetts in the 17th century, how would you have reacted to the banishment of Roger Williams and Anne Hutchinson and the hanging of Mary Dyer?
- If you were a young Wampanoag Indian, would you have joined King Philip in his late 17th century attempt to push the colonial settlers out of the region known as New England, even if you felt it was unlikely to succeed? Explain.

Founding of the 13 Colonies *(cont.)*

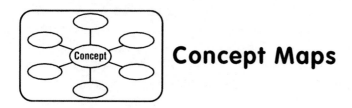

Concept Maps

Develop a concept map for each of the following:

- "City Upon a Hill"
- Dissent
- "Great Migration"
- Tolerance

Venn Diagrams

Roger Williams' Dissent vs. Anne Hutchinson's Dissent: Compare and contrast the actions taken by Roger Williams in 17th-century Massachusetts that put him at odds with Puritan leaders and those taken by Anne Hutchinson during this same period that also led to a clash with Puritan ministers.

Founding of Maryland vs. Founding of Pennsylvania: Compare and contrast the goals and motivation behind the founding and settlement of Maryland and Pennsylvania.

Vee Heuristics

Role of Religion in Colonial Government vs. Role of Religion in the Current Political System: How did society's view of the role of religion in government change from the colonial period to today?

Successes of Original 12 Colonies vs. Failures of the Original 12 Colonies: If you were an advisor to James Oglethorpe, founder of Georgia, the last of the 13 colonies, what successes and failures from the founding of the other 12 colonies would you tell him to keep in mind in the planning of his new colony?

Early Colonial Society

Journal Prompts

- Why were various groups of immigrants attracted to certain regions within the colonies? Why did these patterns of immigration continue throughout American history?

- Why did the colonists turn to African slavery as a form of labor? How did Southern plantation owners justify such a horrible institution?

- Was confrontation between English colonists and Native Americans, such as King Philip's War and Bacon's Rebellion, inevitable? Explain.

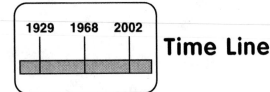

Time Line

Develop a time line listing events relevant to the following themes:

- Confrontations Between Colonists and Native Americans
- Spread of Slavery in the Colonies
- Population Growth of the Major Regions within the Colonies

Decision-Making Scenarios

- If you were a young person living on one of the subsistence farms located in the backcountry region, would you simply give up and move back to England or continue to eke out an existence? Explain.

- If you were a young African slave on a Southern plantation, what would you do to resist and rebel against those who enslave you?

- If you were an indentured servant living in the middle colonies, what would your diary entry read on the first night after your arrival and on the night before you complete your contract of servitude and are given a plot of land? Would you recommend to friends back in England to take the same path as you did to get to America?

Early Colonial Society *(cont.)*

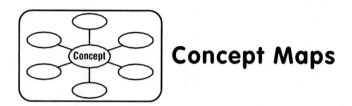

Concept Maps

Develop a concept map for each of the following:

- New England
- Middle Colonies
- Southern Colonies
- Backcountry

Venn Diagrams

New England Village Life vs. Middle Colonies Urban Life: Compare and contrast life in a New England fishing village with that of life in Philadelphia, the largest city in the colonies, located in the middle colonies.

Backcountry Farm Life vs. Southern Colonies Plantation Life: Compare and contrast life on a backcountry family farm with that of life on a Southern plantation.

Vee Heuristics

Positive Aspects of Slave Religion vs. Negative Aspects of Slave Religion: How could religion be used as a source of inspiration for African slaves and a tool of oppression by slaveholders?

Positive Aspects of Slave Family vs. Negative Aspects of Slave Family: How could an African slave's family be both a source of happiness and sorrow?

Maturing Colonial Society

Journal Prompts

- What were the causes of the Salem witchcraft hysteria of the 1690s? Could this ever happen again? Explain.

- Why was the Glorious Revolution in England of such importance in the colonies? What impact did this event have on leading America closer to revolution?

- If you worked as a printing clerk for *Poor Richard's Almanack* and Benjamin Franklin asked you to add a witty saying or piece of advice, what would you write?

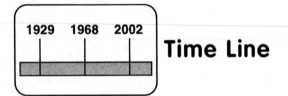

Time Line

Develop a time line listing events relevant to the following themes:

- Early Colonial Period Unrest
- Glorious Revolution
- Early Colonial Culture (Print): Books and Periodicals

Decision-Making Scenarios

- If you were a young farmer living in the Virginia backcountry in the late 17th century, would you have joined Nathaniel Bacon in his revolt against the colonial government? Explain.

- If you were living in late 17th century Salem and your best friend was accused of being a "witch," what would you do?

- If you worked as a colonial newspaper publisher, would you have pointed out the corruption that existed in colonial government, as did John Peter Zenger, even if it might result in losing your job and possibly going to jail? Explain.

Maturing Colonial Society *(cont.)*

Concept Maps

Develop a concept map for each of the following:

- Culture
- Divine Right
- Freedom
- Rebellion

Venn Diagrams

Planters' Perspective vs. Colonial Establishment's Perspective: Compare and contrast Bacon's Rebellion from the perspective of Virginia planters and the Virginia colonial establishment.

Responses to Leisler's Rebellion vs. Responses to Coode's Rebellion: Compare and contrast the response of the colonial elite to Leisler's Rebellion in New York and Coode's Rebellion in Maryland.

Vee Heuristics

Pre-Restoration Relationship Between Monarchy & Colonies vs. Post-Restoration Relationship Between Monarchy & Colonies: How did the relationship between the British monarchy and the Colonies before 1660 differ from their relationship after the Restoration, which witnessed the return of the Stuart monarchy?

Pre-Glorious Revolution British Rule in the Colonies vs. "Constitutional Monarchy" Rule in the Colonies: How did British rule in the Colonies before the Glorious Revolution differ from that which developed in the post-revolution period under a new "constitutional monarchy" in 1689?

The Colonies on the Eve of Revolution

 ## Journal Prompts

- If you attended a Jonathan Edwards-led religious revival in the 1730s, what would you have seen and heard? What impact would it have had on you?

- What are the similarities and differences between colonial education and schooling today?

- How could a figure of the American Enlightenment—such as Cotton Mather, who authored over 450 books on science, history, government, and theology—also have contributed to the hysteria of the Salem witchcraft trials?

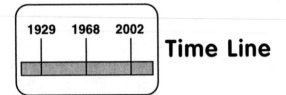 ## Time Line

Develop a time line listing events relevant to the following themes:

- First Great Awakening

- Enlightenment

- Establishment of Colonial Colleges

 ## Decision-Making Scenarios

- A number of colonists, such as John Bartram and John Winthrop III, contributed to the Enlightenment. In what areas do you think you might have been able to contribute to this movement? What impact would your contribution have had on colonial society?

- If you were a member of a colonial assembly in the early 18th century, what would be the first piece of legislation you would submit and why?

- If you were placed in charge of designing the curriculum for one of the first colleges in the colonies, such as Harvard or Yale, what subjects would you have required all students to take? Explain why.

The Colonies on the Eve of Revolution *(cont.)*

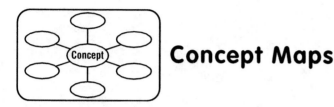

Concept Maps

Develop a concept map for each of the following:

- Education

- Faith

- Inequality

- "Melting Pot"

Venn Diagrams

17ᵗʰ-Century Immigration vs. 18ᵗʰ-Century Immigration: Compare and contrast the motivation and goals of those groups who immigrated to American in the 17ᵗʰ and 18ᵗʰ centuries.

Impact of the Enlightenment vs. Impact of the Great Awakening: Compare and contrast the impact of the Enlightenment and Great Awakening on the impending American Revolution.

Vee Heuristics

Northern Social and Economic Structure vs. Southern Social and Economic Structure: In what ways did the social and economic structure of New England and the Middle Colonies differ from that found in the South and backcountry?

British Perspective on Role of Women vs. American Perspective on Role of Women: How did the British and American colonists differ in their view of the role of women in society?

The Road to Revolution

Journal Prompts

- Although a major plea of the colonists was "no taxation without representation," why was this really not what colonial leaders wanted? If this wasn't what they wanted, why did these leaders make this demand?

- Create a slogan in protest to various acts passed by the British Parliament against the colonies.

- Prioritize the top three events that you believe played the most significant roles in the American colonists' decision to declare independence from England, and discuss why you chose these particular events.

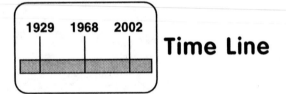

Time Line

Develop a time line listing events relevant to the following themes:

- Colonial Protest
- Seven Years War
- Rise in Colonial Self-Government

Decision-Making Scenarios

- You are a member of the Second Constitutional Convention in Philadelphia in the summer of 1776. What is your reaction when you hear the Declaration of Independence read for the first time on July 2ⁿᵈ at the Philadelphia State House?

- If you were a friend of Abigail Adams, how would you assist her in writing to her husband, John, at the Second Continental Congress? Would you encourage her to be more or less vocal in petitioning him to include the emancipation of women in the Declaration of Independence? Explain.

- If you were the British Prime Minister during the late 18ᵗʰ century, how would you have responded to the colonial protests, such as the Stamp Act Protest? Would you have been more harsh or lenient? Explain.

The Road to Revolution *(cont.)*

Concept Maps

Develop a concept map for each of the following:

- Independence
- Liberty
- Monarchy
- Revolution

Venn Diagrams

British Perspective vs. American Perspective: Compare and contrast how the British and American colonists viewed the events that took place at what became known as the Boston Massacre.

Colonial Newspaper Account vs. British Newspaper Account: Describe how you think the Boston Tea Party was reported in colonial newspapers at the time, and how this event was reported in newspapers back in England.

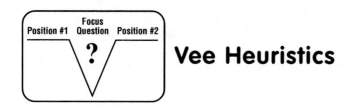

Vee Heuristics

End of One Era vs. Beginning of Another Era: How did the Seven Years War mark both the end of one era in American history and the beginning of another?

Revolution vs. Evolution: Was the American Revolution truly a revolution that lasted only eight years (1763–1776) or an evolutionary event or process that began in 1607 and concluded in 1776?

American Revolution

Journal Prompts

- When is revolution not a justifiable option for a people? Under what circumstances is revolution justified?

- During the American Revolution, Deborah Sampson dressed as a man in order to join the army. What is the significance of this event? What is the role of women today in the military?

- Explain what Thomas Paine meant when he wrote, "These are the times that try men's souls . . ."

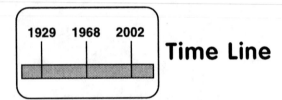

Time Line

Develop a time line listing events relevant to the following themes:

- American Revolution: Northern-Theater Battles

- American Revolution: Southern-Theater Battles

- American Revolution: Western-Theater Battles

Decision-Making Scenarios

- If you were an African slave who was offered the opportunity to fight in the American Revolution on the side of either the British or Americans, which would you choose? Explain.

- If you were a soldier at Valley Forge during the harsh winter of 1777–1778, would you remain with your unit if your military commitment/enlistment ran out or would you return home? Explain.

- If you were a member of American military commander Francis "Swamp Fox" Marion's band of raiders, would you participate in raids against British and Loyalist troops or only British units? Explain.

American Revolution *(cont.)*

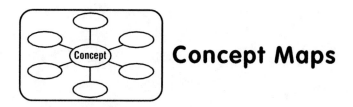 ## **Concept Maps**

Develop a concept map for each of the following:

- Hessians
- Loyalists
- Minute Men
- Patriots

 ## **Venn Diagrams**

British Advantages vs. American Advantages: Compare and contrast the advantages held by the British and Americans in the American Revolution.

British Disadvantages vs. American Disadvantages: Compare and contrast the disadvantages or obstacles that the British and Americans faced in the American Revolution.

 ## **Vee Heuristics**

Patriot Perspective vs. Loyalist Perspective: How did the perspectives of patriots and loyalists differ on whether or not to go to war with England?

British Military Strategy vs. American Military Strategy: How did the military strategy employed by the British military commanders during the American Revolution differ from that of the American military leaders?

Revolutionary Society and Politics

Journal Prompts

- Thomas Paine's *Common Sense* had a tremendous impact on colonial society. In your lifetime, what book has had the greatest impact on American society? Explain.

- When writing the Declaration of Independence, Thomas Jefferson wrestled with whether to include the emancipation of slaves in the document, commenting that slavery was like "having a wolf by the ears." Why did he decide to omit any mention of slavery?

- Rewrite the main passages of the Declaration of Independence, using present-day terms and phrases.

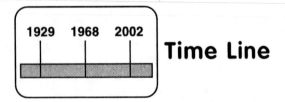

Time Line

Develop a time line listing events relevant to the following themes:

- First Continental Congress
- Second Continental Congress
- Confederation Congress

Decision-Making Scenarios

- If you were a French citizen, why would you side with the Americans and not the British in the American Revolution?

- You are a member of the Continental Congress. Devise a plan of government to get us through the revolution and explain how you would get your plan passed.

- If you were a member of the Second Continental Congress, would you have voted for sending the Olive Branch Petition to King George III? Explain. What would have happened had King George III accepted this offer of peace in 1775?

Revolutionary Society and Politics *(cont.)*

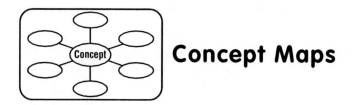

Concept Maps

Develop a concept map for each of the following:

- Articles of Confederation
- *Common Sense*
- Declaration of Independence
- Olive Branch Petition

Venn Diagrams

Conservative Revolution vs. Radical Revolution: Compare and contrast the claim that the American Revolution was both conservative and radical.

First Continental Congress' Role & Accomplishments vs. Second Continental Congress' Role & Accomplishments: Compare and contrast the role and accomplishments of the First Continental Congress of 1774 with those of its successor, the Second Continental Congress that was convened the next year.

Vee Heuristics

American View of the Terms of the Treaty of Paris vs. French View of the Terms of the Treaty of Paris: How did American and French delegates to the Paris peace talks of 1782-1783 differ in their view of how the terms of the peace treaty should be worked out with England?

Why the Americans Won vs. Why the British Lost: How was the American Revolution as much lost by the British as it was won by the Americans?

Constitutional Convention

Journal Prompts

- How would the proceedings and resulting document of the Constitutional Convention have been different had Thomas Jefferson, John Adams, and Patrick Henry been present?

- Why was the issue of separation of church and state so essential to this new democracy?

- Describe the typical delegate to the Constitutional Convention. What significance is there in knowing who attended the convention?

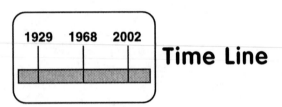

Time Line

Develop a time line listing events relevant to the following themes:

- Drafting of State Constitutions

- Constitutional Convention

- Ratification Process

Decision-Making Scenarios

- If you were hired as a political consultant to oversee the ratification of the Constitution, what would be the focus and strategy of your public relations campaign?

- If you were a delegate at the Constitutional Convention and could add one clause or component to the document and remove one clause or component from the new plan of government, what would you choose for each? Explain.

- If you were put in charge of drafting your state's first constitution, what would be the key components of the document and the structure of the state government?

Constitutional Convention *(cont.)*

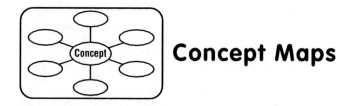 ## Concept Maps

Develop a concept map for each of the following:

- Bill of Rights

- Constitution

- Federalism

- Great Compromise

 ## Venn Diagrams

Articles of Confederation vs. U.S. Constitution: Compare and contrast the role of the central government under the Articles of Confederation and the U.S. Constitution.

Virginia Plan vs. New Jersey Plan: Compare and contrast the features and type of government proposed in the Virginia and New Jersey Plans.

 ## Vee Heuristics

Articles of Confederation = Success vs. Articles of Confederation = Failure: How were the Articles of Confederation both a symbol of success and failure?

Positive Aspect of Compromise vs. Negative Aspect of Compromise: Was the spirit of compromise present at the Constitutional Convention a good or bad component?

Creating a New Republic

Journal Prompts

- Why were slaves and free blacks excluded from the political process in the newly established government?

- Why were Native Americans excluded from the political process in the newly established government?

- What else would you set aside land for in the Land Ordinance of 1785 besides education? What else would you prohibit in the Northwest Ordinance of 1787 besides slavery? Explain both.

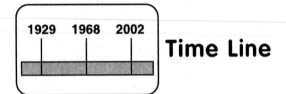

Time Line

Develop a time line listing events relevant to the following themes:

- Opening of the Northwest Territory

- Late 18th Century Relationship and Treaties between the American Government and Native Americans

- Rise and Fall of the Federalist Party

Decision-Making Scenarios

- If you were a friend of Daniel Shays, what would you have done to convince him not to lead his revolt against the government?

- If you were a young surveyor from back East who was sent to the Northwest Territory to help plot out the new townships, what would you write in a letter to your family about the scenic beauty of the region? Would you move your family to the Northwest Territory once your job was finished? Explain.

- If you were a Native American living in the Great Lakes region, what would you do when you started witnessing the migration of thousands of American settlers into what had been for centuries your family's homeland?

Creating a New Republic *(cont.)*

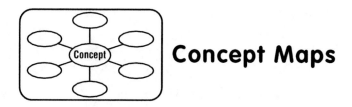

Concept Maps

Develop a concept map for each of the following:

- Federalists
- Anti-Federalists
- Republic
- United States of America

Venn Diagrams

Articles of Confederation vs. U.S. Constitution: Compare and contrast the participation of "common people" in the government during the colonial period with their participation in governance within the new republic.

Colonial Role of Women vs. Role of Women in the New Republic: Compare and contrast the role of women in society and government during the colonial period with the role they assumed in the new republic.

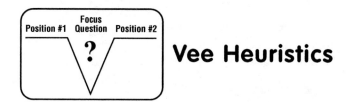

Vee Heuristics

Federalist's View of Power vs. Anti-Federalist's View of Power: How did the Federalists and Anti-Federalists differ in their interpretation of the role of power in a democratic government?

Federalist's View of Liberty vs. Anti-Federalist's View of Liberty: How did the Federalists and Anti-Federalists differ in their interpretation of the role of liberty in a democracy?

The Federalist Era

Journal Prompts

- When Congress asked George Washington to choose a site for the new U.S. Capitol in 1790, why do you think he chose what is today its current location? If that area wasn't available, where would you think would have been the next most logical location? Explain why.

- During the late 18th century, John Adams identified the "five pillars of aristocracy" (birth, wealth, status, talent, and virtue), which he said were necessary requirements for government service. Identify which of these you think are no longer relevant, as well as which ones you think should be added to the list.

- How would the history of the United States have been altered had the Virginia and Kentucky Resolutions been determined to be constitutional?

1929 1968 2002

Time Line

Develop a time line listing events relevant to the following themes:

- Federalists Foreign Policy Accomplishments and Setbacks

- French Revolution

- Internal Conflicts (e.g., Battle of Fallen Timbers, Whiskey Rebellion)

Decision-Making Scenarios

- If you were a foreign policy advisor for President Washington when the French Revolution first broke out in 1789, what position would you suggest the U.S. take? Would your position change in 1793 after King Louis XVI was put to death by guillotine? Explain.

- If you were a newspaper publisher during the Federalist period, what would you write in an editorial when you first became aware of passage of the Alien and Sedition Acts?

- If you were a foreign policy advisor for President Adams when news of the XYZ Affair first broke in 1797, what position would you suggest the U.S. take?

The Federalist Era *(cont.)*

 ## Concept Maps

Develop a concept map for each of the following:

- Alien and Sedition Acts
- Federalist Party
- Virginia and Kentucky Resolutions
- XYZ Affair

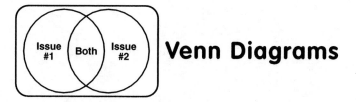 ## Venn Diagrams

Washington Administration vs. Adams Administration: Compare and contrast the accomplishments and setbacks of the George Washington and John Adams administrations.

Pro-French Foreign Policy vs. Pro-British Foreign Policy: Compare and contrast the foreign policy positions advocated by pro-French and pro-British forces in government, in light of events that were going on in Europe during the Federalist period.

 ## Vee Heuristics

Strict Constructionists View vs. Loose Constructionists View: How did the Jeffersonian strict constructionists and Hamiltonian loose constructionists differ in their interpretation of the constitutionality of a national bank?

Whiskey Rebellion = Democracy vs. Whiskey Rebellion = Threat: How did the Whiskey Rebellion of 1791 illustrate both the manifestation of democracy as well as a threat to democracy?

Age of Jefferson

Journal Prompts

- Why is the presidential election of 1800 referred to by historians as the "Revolution of 1800"?

- Why is the Louisiana Purchase considered as one of the most significant events of the 19th century?

- How would the course of history have been altered had Tecumseh and his brother the Prophet been successful in uniting Native Americans in the late 18th and early 19th centuries?

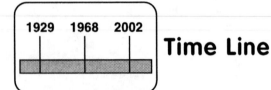

Time Line

Develop a time line listing events relevant to the following themes:

- Major Supreme Court Rulings under Chief Justice John Marshall

- Jefferson Administration Foreign Policy Accomplishments and Setbacks

- Louisiana Purchase and Louisiana Territory Exploration

Decision-Making Scenarios

- If you were in the position of Alexander Hamilton, who basically could use his influence to determine who would be named president following the 1800 presidential election electoral tie, would you have chosen Thomas Jefferson or Aaron Burr? Explain.

- What would one of your diary entries read like if you were a member of Lewis and Clark's Corps of Discovery exploring the Louisiana Territory for President Jefferson?

- If you were a member of President Jefferson's cabinet during the Chesapeake-Leopard incident of 1807, what action would you have recommended he take?

Age of Jefferson *(cont.)*

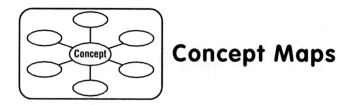 ## Concept Maps

Develop a concept map for each of the following:

- Agrarian Democracy
- Louisiana Purchase
- Midnight Justices
- Jeffersonian-Republican Party

 ## Venn Diagrams

Federalist Administrations vs. Jefferson Administration: Compare and contrast the accomplishments and setbacks of the Federalist administrations of Washington and Adams with those of Thomas Jefferson's two terms of office.

Agrarian Vision of America vs. Industrial Vision of America: Compare and contrast the benefits and drawbacks of Thomas Jefferson's agrarian vision for America with the industrial vision for America advocated by Alexander Hamilton.

 ## Vee Heuristics

Federalist's View of Purchase vs. Republican View of Purchase: How did the Federalists and Republicans differ in their views of the Louisiana Purchase?

Jefferson's Perspective vs. Marshall's Perspective: How did President Thomas Jefferson and Chief Justice John Marshall differ in their interpretation of the Constitution and in their view of the role of government?

Mr. Madison's War of 1812

Journal Prompts

- Was the War of 1812 justified? When, if ever, is war justified?

- What would have happened had the Hartford Convention been held one year earlier? Is it ever acceptable to criticize the government during wartime? Explain.

- Why did the American delegation agree to the terms of the peace treaty outlined at Ghent in 1814 if they didn't address the issues that led to the outbreak of war?

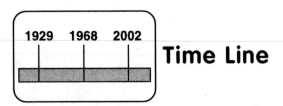

Time Line

Develop a time line listing events relevant to the following themes:

- War of 1812: Events that Led to the Outbreak of War

- War of 1812: Ground War

- War of 1812: Naval War

Decision-Making Scenarios

- If you were a member of Congress in 1931, would you vote for or against making Francis Scott Key's "Star Spangled Banner," penned at Fort McHenry in 1814, the national anthem? Explain why you would either vote in favor of the "Star Spangled Banner," or if you oppose this decision, what song you would substitute and why?

- If you were a newspaper publisher during the early 19th century, how would you have reported the assault on and destruction of Washington, D. C., by British troops in 1814?

- If you were a member of Andrew Jackson's military unit at the Battle of New Orleans, what would you write in a letter back home to your family in January 1815?

Mr. Madison's War of 1812 *(cont.)*

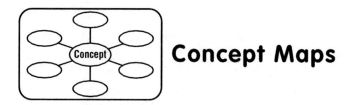

Concept Maps

Develop a concept map for each of the following:

- Hartford Convention
- "Star Spangled Banner"
- War Hawks
- War of 1812

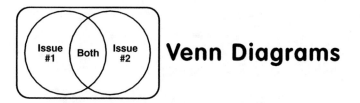

Venn Diagrams

British Advantages vs. American Advantages: Compare and contrast the advantages held by the British and Americans in the War of 1812.

British Disadvantages vs. American Disadvantages: Compare and contrast the disadvantages or obstacles that the British and Americans faced in the War of 1812.

Vee Heuristics

Anti-British Factors vs. Pro-French Factors: How was America's decision to go to war with England in 1812 influenced as much by anti-British feelings as it was by pro-French sentiments?

"Father of the Constitution" vs. President of the United States: How did the role James Madison played in the drafting of the Constitution differ from his role as president? Also, what has been the impact of each of these roles in shaping Madison's legacy?

The Virginia Dynasty and Era of Good Feelings

Journal Prompts

- How did the government and court promote economic growth during the "Era of Good Feelings"?

- Why do you believe that four of the first five presidents of the United States were from Virginia? Why were George Washington's political views so much different than those of Virginia's other native sons? Did any state or region dominate American presidential politics in any other period of American history?

- How did the American public receive the Monroe Doctrine when it was first issued in 1823? How would it be received today? Explain why you believe the public reception would be either the same or different.

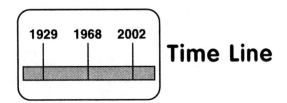

Time Line

Develop a time line listing events relevant to the following themes:

- Foreign Policy Accomplishments and Setbacks of the Virginia Dynasty
- Western Expansion during the Virginia Dynasty
- Rise and Fall of Nationalism During the "Era of Good Feelings"

Decision-Making Scenarios

- If you were a member of President Monroe's state department, what would you have suggested to Secretary of State John Quincy Adams that he include in the Monroe Doctrine, and what would you have suggested he remove?

- If you were writing the history of the "Era of Good Feelings," what label would you apply to this period in American history that more truly reflects the events and status of the nation at this time? Support your historical label with specific historical facts or evidence.

- If you were a newspaper publisher during the early 19th century, would you praise or criticize President Monroe for his support of the attempt to create the colony of Liberia, whose capital was named Monrovia as a result, in Africa for ex-slaves?

The Virginia Dynasty and Era of Good Feelings *(cont.)*

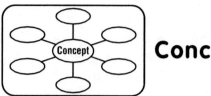

Concept Maps

Develop a concept map for each of the following:

- Era of Good Feelings
- Monroe Doctrine
- Nationalism
- Virginia Dynasty

Venn Diagrams

Jefferson Administration vs. Madison Administration: Compare and contrast the accomplishments and setbacks of President Thomas Jefferson with those of his successor, James Madison.

Monroe Administration vs. Jefferson & Madison Administrations: Compare and contrast the accomplishments and setbacks of President James Monroe with those of the other chief executives of the Virginia Dynasty.

Vee Heuristics

Positive Legacy of Compromise vs. Negative Legacy of Compromise: How was the Missouri Compromise both a positive example of interregional compromise as well as a negative precedent that paved the way for even greater division and sectionalism?

Era of Good Feelings vs. Era of Bad Feelings: How was the post-War of 1812 period in American history both an "Era of Good Feelings" as well as an "Era of Bad Feelings"?

The Jacksonian Period

Journal Prompts

- Political mudslinging during the 1828 presidential election campaign reached an all-time low, with Adams' camp accusing Jackson of being a murderer and adulterer and the Jackson campaign staff accusing Adams of gambling in the White House. Is such mudslinging inevitable in presidential campaigns, or has society grown tired of such a practice? Explain.

- What would have happened had South Carolina's nullification of a federal law and threat of secession been ignored by President Jackson in 1832? Was there any connection between South Carolina's threat of secession in 1832 and actual secession in 1860? Explain.

- How could the government justify the 1838 removal of nearly 15,000 Native Americans from their homelands in the southeastern United States and forced march to "Indian Territory," all of which resulted in the death of 4,000 Cherokees? Is there any way this wrong could or should be righted today?

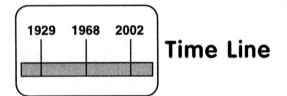

Time Line

Develop a time line listing events relevant to the following themes:

- The First 19th Century Indian Removal
- History of Political Parties in the First Half of the 19th Century
- Rise of Jacksonian Democracy

Decision-Making Scenarios

- If you were hired as a political consultant to oversee the 1828 Andrew Jackson presidential campaign, how would you integrate the events of the 1824 presidential election into your current campaign strategy?

- If you were a newspaper reporter assigned to cover the inauguration of Andrew Jackson in 1829, what would you have wrote concerning the events of the day and the significance of Jackson's election?

- If you were a member of Congress in 1830 during the debate over the proposed Indian Removal Act, what would you have said in a speech on the floor of the House concerning this piece of legislation, which would eventually lead to the event known as the "Trail of Tears"?

The Jacksonian Period *(cont.)*

Concept Maps

Develop a concept map for each of the following:

- "Common Man"
- New Democracy
- Nullification
- "Trail of Tears"

Venn Diagrams

National Republican Party vs. Democratic Party: Compare and contrast the political beliefs of the two new political parties, the National Republicans and Democrats, which replaced the old Republican Party by 1828.

Adams Administration vs. Jackson Administration: Compare and contrast the accomplishments and setbacks of President John Quincy Adams with those of his successor, Andrew Jackson.

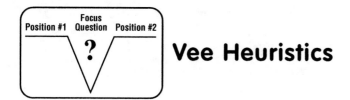

Vee Heuristics

Daniel Webster's View of Sovereignty vs. Robert Hayne's View of Sovereignty: How did Daniel Webster and Robert Hayne differ in their view of sovereignty, as expressed in their famous debate on the floor of the U.S. Senate?

General Andrew Jackson vs. President Andrew Jackson: How did Andrew Jackson's image as a military leader and war hero differ from that of his presidency?

Search for Utopia

Journal Prompts

- Why did so many Americans go in search of utopia in the form of the various communities that were founded in the first half of the 19th century? Has this same desire and search appeared during other periods of American history? Explain.

- Why did other figures in history, such as Gandhi and Martin Luther King, Jr., emulate Henry David Thoreau's actions and quote his writings concerning civil disobedience?

- What led to the downfall of most of the 19th century utopian communities? Why did some of the religious denominations and communities founded during this period survive?

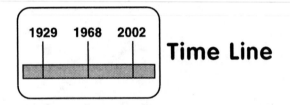

Time Line

Develop a time line listing events relevant to the following themes:

- 19th Century Founding and Growth of Religious Denominations
- Rise and Fall of Utopian Communities
- Second Great Awakening

Decision-Making Scenarios

- If you were to choose to become a member of one of the utopian communities founded in the 19th century, which one would you choose and why?

- If you followed Joseph Smith to Nauvoo, Illinois, during the early 19th century and witnessed his murder there, would you have followed Brigham Young westward to Utah or returned to your home back east? Explain.

- If you were a transcendentalist writer during the early 19th century, what societal topic would you have written about and what would you have hoped would result from your writings?

Search for Utopia *(cont.)*

 ## Concept Maps

Develop a concept map for each of the following:

- 2ⁿᵈ Great Awakening
- Civil Disobedience
- Utopia
- Transcendentalism

 ## Venn Diagrams

First Great Awakening vs. Second Great Awakening: Compare and contrast the leaders, messages, events, and legacies of the First and Second Great Awakenings.

Oneida, New York vs. New Harmony, Indiana: Compare and contrast the goals, methods, successes, and setbacks experienced by John Noyes and his followers at Oneida with those of Robert Owen and his followers at New Harmony.

 ## Vee Heuristics

Whitman's View of American society vs. Poe's View of American society: How did the poets Walt Whitman and Edgar Allan Poe differ in their view of American society and democracy?

Religious Leaders' Approach vs. Utopian Community Leaders' Approach: How did religious leaders and utopian community founders differ in their approach to addressing the problems facing American society during the early 19ᵗʰ century?

Abolitionist and Anti-Slavery Movements

Journal Prompts

- What is the meaning of the following Ralph Waldo Emerson 1941 quote, "If you put a chain around the neck of a slave, the other end fastens itself around your own"?

- Why did Harriet Beecher Stowe's *Uncle Tom's Cabin* have such an impact on the abolitionist movement? What other books in American history have had such a tremendous impact on society?

- Why did it take over two centuries from the time in which slavery was first introduced in America for a well-organized and relatively effective abolitionist movement to take form? Would such a movement ever have come about if slavery had been legal in every state of the Union? Explain.

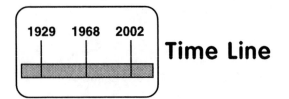

Time Line

Develop a time line listing events relevant to the following themes:

- Spread of Slavery in the South

- Growth of the Abolitionist Movement in the United States

- Growth of the Anti-Slavery Movement Throughout the World

Decision-Making Scenarios

- If you went with Harriet Tubman on one of her 19 trips to the South to help bring slaves North to freedom on the Underground Railroad, how would you justify risking your life to undertake this daring venture in a letter to your family back home?

- If you were on the staff of William Lloyd Garrison's *The Liberator* and learned that your boss was planning to publicly burn a copy of the Constitution in protest over slavery—which he did in 1854 proclaiming it a "covenant with death"—what would you tell him if he asked you if he should do this?

- If you were a newspaper reporter sent to cover an anti-slavery meeting in which Sojourner Truth and Frederick Douglass spoke, what would you write for your article the next day?

Abolitionist and Anti-Slavery Movements *(cont.)*

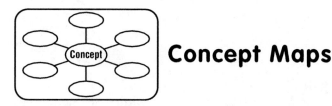

Concept Maps

Develop a concept map for each of the following:

- Abolitionism
- Emancipation
- "Peculiar Institution"
- Underground Railroad

Venn Diagrams

ACS Founders' Motives & Objectives vs. Abolitionists' Motives & Objectives: Compare and contrast the motivation and objectives of the founders of the American Colonization Society (ACS), established in 1816, with those of the abolitionists.

Northern Anti-Slavery & Abolitionist Movement vs. Southern Anti-Slavery & Abolitionist Movement: Compare and contrast the strategies and impact of the anti-slavery and abolitionist movements in the North and South.

Vee Heuristics

Abolitionists' Tactics vs. Radical Abolitionists' Tactics: How did abolitionists, such as Frederick Douglass, and radical abolitionists, such as David Waker, differ in the tactics they advocated for bringing about an end to slavery?

Constitutional Protection of Slavery vs. Constitutional Abolition of Slavery: How was the U.S. Constitution both a document that was used to initially protect slavery and later the tool used to gain freedom for all Americans?

America in Transition

Journal Prompts

- What factors contributed to the spirit of invention (as evidenced by Samuel F.B. Morse's telegraph, Elias Howe's sewing machine, Cyrus McCormick's reaper, etc.) that seemed to characterize America during the early 19th century?

- Why did America experience a three-fold increase in immigration during the mid 19th century? Why did some nativists oppose such immigration when they themselves were descended from immigrants?

- Was the shift from a Jefferson agrarian America to a Hamiltonian industrial America inevitable? Explain.

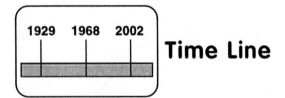

Time Line

Develop a time line listing events relevant to the following themes:

- Rise of America's Early 19th-Century Transportation Network
- Growth of Industry in the Early 19th Century
- Early-19th-Century Urbanization

Decision-Making Scenarios

- If you were a newspaper reporter sent to cover the maiden voyage of Robert Fulton's steam-powered riverboat *Clemont*, what would you write in your article about the significance of this event?

- If you were a worker in a Lowell cotton mill, what would you include in your first letter home? Would you tell your parents that you wanted to go back home or stay? Explain.

- What would one of your diary entries read like if you were a young person living in New England during the early 19th century who had just witnessed his or her first whaling voyage?

America in Transition *(cont.)*

Concept Maps

Develop a concept map for each of the following:

- American System
- Lowell and Waltham System
- Mass Production
- Nativism

Venn Diagrams

Urbanization Factors vs. Industrialization Factors: Compare and contrast the factors that contributed to the growth of American cities and industry in the early 19th century.

Early-19th-Century Union Objectives & Tactics vs. Early-21st-Century Union Objectives & Tactics: Compare and contrast the objectives and tactics used by trade unions during the early 19th century with those of today.

Vee Heuristics

Lowell Mills = Independence vs. Lowell Mills = Exploitation: How did the Lowell cotton mills of the early 19th century serve both to illustrate greater independence for women as well as further exploitation of women during this period?

Economic Specialization = Blessing vs. Economic Specialization = Curse: How was economic specialization both a blessing and a curse for many urban areas and regions within the United States during the early 19th century?

Slavery and the Old South

Journal Prompts

- Why did so many non-slave holding, white Southerners, who represented 75 percent of the region's population, still support slavery?

- What is the meaning of the following Thomas Jefferson analogy: "Slavery is like holding a wolf by the ears"?

- Why didn't more Southerners recognize, as did Hinton Helper, the negative impact the dependence on slavery had on the economic growth of the region? Were economic attacks on slavery more effective than moral arguments in persuading Southerners to abandon the institution? Explain.

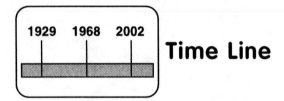

Time Line

Develop a time line listing events relevant to the following themes:

- Dependeney on Slave Labor during the 19th Century

- Growth of Cotton Production during the 19th Century

- Slave Revolts and Rebellions

Decision-Making Scenarios

- If you were an author who was opposed to slavery, living in the South during the early 19th century, what would you write to counter the bogus theories that were promulgated by slaveholders to justify slavery (e.g., Herrenvolk Democracy, Polygenesis)?

- If you were a young slave living on a plantation in the South, would you attempt to run away on the Underground Railroad if given the chance, knowing that the penalty might be mutilation or death; or would you endure your captivity and remain with your family? Explain.

- If you were the president of the United States during the early 19th century, what would you do to bring about an end to slavery? Would your plan have worked? Explain.

Slavery and the Old South *(cont.)*

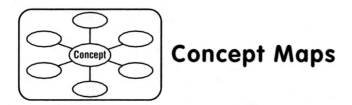

Concept Maps

Develop a concept map for each of the following:

- King Cotton

- "Necessary Evil"

- Plantation

- Slave Codes

Venn Diagrams

Slavery in the South vs. Wage Labor in the North: Compare and contrast factors that led to the increased demand for slaves in the South and wage labor in the North.

Status of Free Blacks vs. Status of Slaves: Compare and contrast the economic, political, and social status of free blacks and slaves during the 19th century.

Vee Heuristics

Southern Slaves' Hardships vs. Northern Laborers' Hardships: How did the hardships endured by slaves in the South differ from those of factory or mill workers in the North?

Positive Effect of King Cotton vs. Negative Effect of King Cotton: How was "King Cotton" an economic double-edged sword for the South during the 19th century?

Age of Reform

Journal Prompts

• Why were so many women's-rights leaders, such as Lucy Stone and the Grimke sisters, also members of the anti-slavery movement during the 19th century?

• Can reforms ever occur naturally in society, or do they always require the efforts of key individuals, such as Dorothea Dix and Horace Mann, to open our eyes to the problem first? Explain.

• Why did the Seneca Falls Women's Convention delegates choose to mirror their "Declarations of Sentiments" after the Declaration of Independence? Was this analogy accurate? Explain.

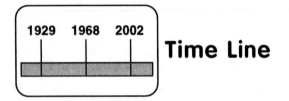

Time Line

Develop a time line listing events relevant to the following themes:

• Rise of the Women's Rights Movement

• 19th and 20th Century Temperance/Prohibition Movement

• Growth of Social Reform Movements

Decision-Making Scenarios

• If you accompanied Dorothea Dix on her visits to American jails and prisons during the 19th century, what evidence would you include in your report to a state legislature in your petition for reform?

• If you were a hearing- or visually-impaired child growing up in 19th century America, how would you respond to the news that Thomas Hopkins Gallaudet had established a school for deaf students or that Samuel Gridley Howe had done the same for blind students?

• If you were one of the women delegates (such as Lucretia Mott) who traveled to the London Anti-Slavery Convention of 1840, only to be denied a seat, what would you have written in a letter to your colleagues back in the United States?

Age of Reform *(cont.)*

Concept Maps

Develop a concept map for each of the following:

- Social Justice
- Reform
- Suffrage
- Temperance

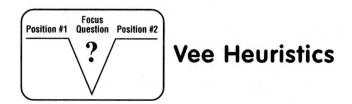

Venn Diagrams

19ᵗʰ-Century View of Manifest Destiny vs. 21ˢᵗ-Century View of Manifest Destiny: Compare and contrast the way most Americans reacted to the doctrine of Manifest Destiny in the 19ᵗʰ century with how it is perceived today.

Immigrants' Motivation vs. Pioneers' Motivation: Compare and contrast the motivation of those individuals who migrated to the "New World" during the 17th century with the motives of those Americans who made the trek westward from their homes back east during the 19ᵗʰ century.

Vee Heuristics

Pop Culture Portrayal of Native American vs. Accurate Portrayal of Native Americans: How did the portrayal of Native Americans in films, television programs, and books differ from the reality of American Indian life during the 19ᵗʰ century?

Northern View of Westward Migration & Statehood vs. Southern View of Westward Migration & Statehood: How did government and economic leaders in North and the South differ in the way they perceived of westward migration and eventual statehood?

Westward Expansion

Journal Prompts

- Why has the American West been such a popular topic with authors and filmmakers over the past century?

- Would California have developed as quickly had it not been for the discovery of gold at Sutter's mill? Why did Nevada not experience the same rapid population increase?

- If so many pioneers lost their lives during their westward trek, why did this not deter others from making the same trip?

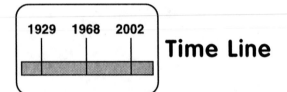

Time Line

Develop a time line listing events relevant to the following themes:

- Development of Famous Trails Westward
- Mining in the West
- Mormon Trek to the West

Decision-Making Scenarios

- If you were a pioneer making your westward trek, what would you write in your diary on the day you departed from your original home and on the day you arrived at your final destination?

- If you were a young person who traveled west during the "Gold Rush" and came up empty-handed, would you remain in California or go back home? Explain.

- If you were a young Native American living in the west during the 19th century, what would you do when you spotted a wagon train of pioneers who were attempting to settle on your land?

Westward Expansion *(cont.)*

Concept Maps

Develop a concept map for each of the following:

- American West
- "Forty-Niner"
- Manifest Destiny
- Pioneer

Venn Diagrams

Utopian Community Leaders vs. Social Reform Movement Leaders: Compare and contrast the goals and activities of utopian community leaders and social reform movement leaders during the 19th century.

Abolitionist Movement vs. Women's-Rights Movement: Compare and contrast the goals and tactics of leaders of the abolitionist and women's rights movements.

Vee Heuristics

Status of Women in the Early National Period vs. Status of Women in the Antebellum Period: How did the status women held in American society during the antebellum period differ from that of the early national period?

Government = Problem vs. Government = Solution: How was government perceived by social reformers as being both part of the problem and part of the solution during the 19th century?

Mexican War

Journal Prompts

- Why was the rally cry "Remember the Alamo" so effective in drumming up support during the Mexican War?

- Why did some Americans, such as Henry David Thoreau, protest the Mexican War?

- Would passage of the Wilmot Proviso in 1846 have delayed or expedited the start of the Civil War? Explain.

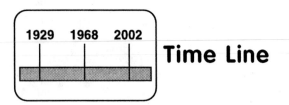

Time Line

Develop a time line listing events relevant to the following themes:

- Texas Independence
- Mexican War
- Acquisition of Western Territories

Decision-Making Scenarios

- If you were a member of Congress in 1846, would you have voted for Abraham Lincoln's "Spot Resolution"? Explain.

- If you were a young newspaper reporter sent to cover the Mexican War, what military battles and leaders would you identify in your article as being instrumental to America's success?

- What would one of your diary entries read like if you were a soldier who was fighting alongside Davy Crockett and Jim Bowie at the Alamo in 1835?

Mexican War *(cont.)*

Concept Maps

Develop a concept map for each of the following:

- Alamo

- Bear Flag Republic

- "Fifty-Four Forty or Fight"

- Treaty of Guadalupe-Hidalgo

Venn Diagrams

Mexican War vs. War of 1812: Compare and contrast the causes, consequences, and significance of the Mexican War with the other 19th-century contest, the War of 1812.

Mexico Advantages & Disadvantages vs. U.S. Advantages & Disadvantages: Compare and contrast the advantages and disadvantages held by Mexico and the United States during the Mexican War.

Vee Heuristics

Mexican Government Account vs. U.S. Government Account: How did the Mexican and American governments differ in their account of the events that occurred at the Alamo?

Mexican Government Account vs. U.S. Government Account: How did the Mexican and American governments differ in their account of the events that led to the outbreak of the Mexican War?

Popular Sovereignty Question

Journal Prompts

- How was America's victory in the Mexican War a cause of both immediate national celebration and long-term anguish?

- How has the principle of "popular sovereignty" emerged in previous events from American history, although it may have been called something different? Why did it become such an explosive issue in the decade preceding the Civil War?

- If the North and the South had agreed to extending the Missouri Compromise line of 36–30' to the Pacific Ocean, would there have been as much regional tension and violence during the 1850s? Explain. What impact would this have had on the start of the Civil War?

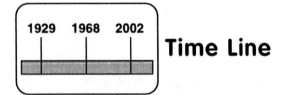

Time Line

Develop a time line listing events relevant to the following themes:

- "Young America" Movement
- "Bleeding Kansas"
- Antebellum Congressional Compromise

Decision-Making Scenarios

- If you were a member of Congress in 1854, what would you have said on the floor of the House when it was your turn to speak on the proposed Kansas-Nebraska Act?

- If you were an abolitionist, what would you write in your newspaper concerning the "Free Soil Movement"? Would you praise or condemn the leaders of the movement? Explain.

- If you were a Supreme Court justice in 1857 and were assigned to draft the dissenting opinion of the Dred Scott vs. Sanford case, what would you write?

Popular Sovereignty Question *(cont.)*

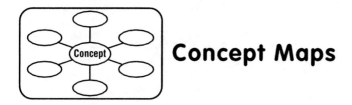

Concept Maps

Develop a concept map for each of the following:

- Compromise of 1850
- "Fire-Eaters"
- Free-Soil Movement
- Popular Sovereignty

Venn Diagrams

Northern Concessions in the Compromise of 1850 vs. Southern Concessions in the Compromise of 1850: Compare and contrast the concessions made to the North and South in the Compromise of 1850.

Dred Scott Decision vs. Freeport Doctrine: Compare and contrast the differing positions on the status of slaves in territories as expressed by the Supreme Court in their 1857 Dred Scott decision and Stephen Douglas in the 1858 Freeport Doctrine.

Vee Heuristics

Northern View of Gadsden Purchase vs. Southern View of Gadsden Purchase: How did the North and South differ in how they viewed the Gadsden Purchase of 1853?

Northern View of Kansas-Nebraska Act vs. Southern View of Kansas-Nebraska Act: How did the pro-slavery and anti-slavery factions in America differ in their view of the 1854 Kansas-Nebraska Act?

The Road to War

Journal Prompts

- Why did it take so long for the nation to recognize what Abraham Lincoln prophetically stated in 1858: "A house divided against itself cannot stand"?

- Which candidate would have won the 1860 presidential election had the Democratic Party not split? Would this have delayed the start of the Civil War?

- Would as many states have seceded from the Union by the time of Lincoln's inauguration in March 1861 (seven of the eleven states had already deserted) if President Buchanan had employed some type of military action? Explain.

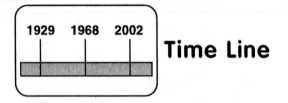

Time Line

Develop a time line listing events relevant to the following themes:

- Rise of the Republican Party
- Life of Abraham Lincoln
- 1860 Political Party Conventions, Campaign, and Election

Decision-Making Scenarios

- If you lived in a region of the United States free of slavery and had just read of the horrors of the "peculiar institution" in Harriet Beecher Stowe's 1852 book *Uncle Tom's Cabin,* what would you do?

- If your were an abolitionist, would you have commended or condemned John Brown for his 1856 attack on the pro-slavery town of Pottawatomie Creek, Kansas, which resulted in the death of five settlers? Explain.

- If you were a newspaper reporter sent to cover the 1858 Lincoln-Douglas Debates, what would you write about the "rail-splitting politician"? Explain.

The Road to War *(cont.)*

Concept Maps

Develop a concept map for each of the following:

- Freeport Doctrine

- Fugitive Slave Law

- "God's Angry Man"

- Secession

Venn Diagrams

Northern View of Secession vs. Southern View of Secession: Compare and contrast the way the North and South viewed the secession of South Carolina in 1860.

Compromise as Prevention vs. Compromise as Catalyst: Compare and contrast how compromise both prevented and contributed to the outbreak of the Civil War.

Vee Heuristics

Northern View of Brooks-Summer Incident vs. Southern View of Brooks-Summer Incident: How did the North and South differ in their interpretations of the May 1856 Preston Brooks and Charles Summer incident?

Northern View of John Brown's Raid vs. Southern View of John Brown's Raid: How did abolitionists and proponents of slavery differ in their view of events that occurred at Harpers Ferry, Virginia, in October 1859 and the resulting hanging of John Brown?

The Civil War: Home Front

Journal Prompts

- Why is the Civil War the most written about topic in American history?

- Was Abraham Lincoln justified in suspending the privilege of the writ of habeas corpus during the Civil War? Explain.

- Do you agree with some notable historians who rank Abraham Lincoln as the greatest president in American history? Explain.

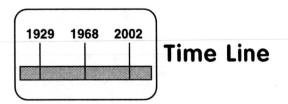

Time Line

Develop a time line listing events relevant to the following themes:

- Role of Women in the Civil War

- Civil War Era Elections and Politics

- Civil War Finance and Economics

Decision-Making Scenarios

- If you lived in the South during the Civil War and were opposed to slavery, would you still support the Confederacy? Explain.

- If you lived in the North during the Civil War and were drafted, what would you do when you found out that wealthy men had been paying for draft substitutes or purchasing exemptions?

- If you worked with Clara Barton or Dr. Elizabeth Blackwell in a Civil War nursing station, what would a typical day's diary entry read like?

The Civil War: Home Front *(cont.)*

 ## Concept Maps

Develop a concept map for each of the following:

- Border States
- Emancipation Proclamation
- Gettysburg Address
- Trent Affair

 ## Venn Diagrams

U.S. President Lincoln vs. C.S.A. President Davis: Compare and contrast the leadership styles, accomplishments, and setbacks of Abraham Lincoln and Jefferson Davis.

Border States' Union Allegiances vs. Border States' Southern Allegiances: Compare and contrast the conflicting allegiances of border states' residents during the Civil War.

 ## Vee Heuristics

Slavery as *the* Cause of the Civil War vs. Slavery as One of Many Causes of the Civil War: Was slavery the primary cause of the Civil War or just one of many factors that led to the bloody conflict?

Emancipation Proclamation = Courageous vs. Emancipation Proclamation = Not Courageous Enough: Why do some consider the Emancipation Proclamation to be a bold and courageous move by President Lincoln while others criticize him for not being daring and courageous enough?

The Civil War: Battlefield

Journal Prompts

- Why did the British government remain neutral during the Civil War? How would the course of the Civil War have been different had England militarily supported the Confederacy?

- Were General William Tecumseh Sherman's "scorched earth" military tactics necessary to bring about an end to the Civil War? Explain. How did his "March to the Sea" both expedite the end of the Civil War and delay the post-war healing?

- Should overly cautious Civil War military leaders, such as General George McClellan, have been commended or criticized? Did they save more lives by not knowingly exposing their troops to excessive risks that would have produced incredibly high casualty rates; or did they prolong the war, thereby increasing the death toll due to their hesitancy?

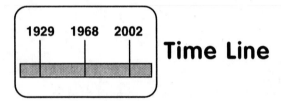

Time Line

Develop a time line listing events relevant to the following themes:

- Civil War: Ground Battles

- Civil War: Naval Battles

- Civil War: Battlefield Accomplishments of African Americans

Decision-Making Scenarios

- If you were a young Confederate soldier who had just witnessed the Confederate surrender at Vicksburg in 1863, what would you tell your family in a letter home?

- If you were a young Union soldier in General Sherman's military unit and had just witnessed the destruction of Atlanta in 1864, what would you tell your family in a letter home?

- If you were one of the 200,000 African-American soldiers who fought for the Union during the Civil War, what would you do when you found out that white troops earned more money, that only white officers could command your unit, and that the Confederacy would execute you if you were captured?

The Civil War: Battlefield *(cont.)*

Concept Maps

Develop a concept map for each of the following:

- Appomattox Courthouse

- Antietam

- Fort Sumter

- Gettysburg

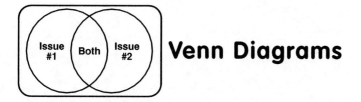

Venn Diagrams

Union Advantages vs. Confederacy Advantages: Compare and contrast the advantages held by the Union and Confederacy during the Civil War.

Union Disadvantages vs. Confederacy Disadvantages: Compare and contrast the disadvantages or obstacles that the Union and Confederacy faced during the Civil War.

Vee Heuristics

Union Strategy & Tactics vs. Confederacy Strategy & Tactics: How did the military strategy and tactics employed by the Union and Confederacy during the Civil War differ?

General Grant's Approach to Warfare vs. General Lee's Approach to Warfare: How did General Ulysses S. Grant's and General Robert E. Lee's approach to warfare differ?

Aftermath of the Civil War

Journal Prompts

- How might events that occurred following the end of the Civil War have been different had Abraham Lincoln escaped the assassin's bullet? Did his death have a greater impact on the North or South? Explain.

- What types of wounds (besides physical ones) had to heal in the North and South after the Civil War? How could the healing process have been made any quicker and easier?

- Why do you believe General Ulysses S. Grant was so polite and lenient toward General Robert E. Lee during the meeting at Appomattox Court House in 1865? Would you have behaved in the same manner if you were Grant? Explain.

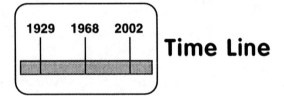

Time Line

Develop a time line listing events relevant to the following themes:

- Lincoln Assassination Plot
- Diplomatic Negotiations that Led to the End of the Civil War
- Demobilization of the Military

Decision-Making Scenarios

- If you were president of the United States in 1865, what three questions or issues would you prioritize at the top of your list of matters that must be addressed? Explain why.

- If you were a reporter assigned to cover the funeral of Abraham Lincoln, what would you write concerning his contribution to the nation and his legacy?

- If you were one of the millions of freed African slaves, or freedmen, what would you do? Would you stay and continue to work the same land as a sharecropper or move somewhere else? Explain.

Aftermath of the Civil War *(cont.)*

Concept Maps

Develop a concept map for each of the following:

- Black Codes

- Demobilization

- Freedmen

- Sharecroppers

Venn Diagrams

Civil War Destruction vs. American Revolution, War of 1812, & Mexican War Destruction: Compare and contrast the death and destruction that resulted from the Civil War with all other wars the United States had fought.

Post-Civil War Emotional Climate in the North vs. Post-Civil War Emotional Climate in the South: Compare and contrast the mood of the people or emotional climate in the North and South immediately following the end of the Civil War.

Vee Heuristics

Destruction & Devastation of the South vs. Destruction & Devastation of the North: How did the destruction and devastation that occurred in the South during the Civil War differ from that experienced by the North?

Lincoln's Plan for Reconstruction vs. Johnson's Plan for Reconstruction: How did Abraham Lincoln's plan for Reconstruction differ from that of his successor, Andrew Johnson?

Reconstruction

Journal Prompts

- Which of the Reconstruction-era amendments do you believe brought about the greatest change in American society? In light of what occurred after Reconstruction, what other amendments do you believe should have been passed?

- Could the government have secured equal rights for the newly freed African-American slaves without the use of military troops, as occurred under the Military Reconstruction Act of 1867; or was the use of armed force an absolute necessity?

- Do you believe President Lincoln's or Johnson's plans for Reconstruction would have been any more effective than the Congressional plan that was implemented? Explain. If you could have devised your own plan for Reconstruction, what would you have included?

1929	1968	2002

Time Line

Develop a time line listing events relevant to the following themes:

- Reconstruction Amendments and Civil Rights Laws

- Political Rise and Fall of Freedom

- Reconstruction Era Congressional and Presidential Elections

Decision-Making Scenarios

- If you were a member of Congress during Reconstruction, would you have voted in favor of President Andrew Johnson's impeachment? Explain.

- If you were a longtime abolitionist who got to see the swearing in of the first African Americans to the United States Congress during Reconstruction, what would you write in your diary about that event and your emotions?

- If you were a white Southerner who had witnessed the influx of Northern carpetbaggers and Union troops into your community during Reconstruction, how would you feel? What would your reaction be to Southern scalawags who cooperated with these individuals?

Reconstruction *(cont.)*

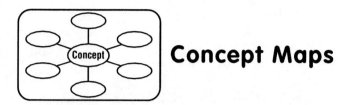

Concept Maps

Develop a concept map for each of the following:

- Carpetbagger
- Radical Republicans
- Reconstruction
- Scalawag

Venn Diagrams

Northern View of Johnson vs. Southern View of Johnson: Compare and contrast the way the North and South perceived President Andrew Johnson.

Presidential Reconstruction Plans vs. Congressional Reconstruction Plan: Compare and contrast the two presidential plans for Reconstruction with that developed by the Radical Republicans in Congress.

Vee Heuristics

View of Former Confederate Leaders = Forgiveness vs. View of Former Confederate Leaders = Revenge: How did Americans differ in their view of what should happen to the former military and political leaders of the Confederacy, and what was their rationale for each position?

Abolitionists' View of Reconstruction vs. Women's Rights Leaders' View of Reconstruction: How did former abolitionist leaders and women's-rights leaders differ in their view of rights bestowed upon freed men during Reconstruction?

Farmer's Revolt

Journal Prompts

- Why did it take until the late 19th century for farmers to establish economic and political alliances/parties? Would farmers have been more successful if they had attempted to create these economic and political organizations decades earlier? Explain.

- If so many of the Populist Party's 19th-century political and economic proposals were eventually adopted by the federal and many state governments, why did the Populist Party collapse after just a few years?

- What would Thomas Jefferson have thought of the status of his "Agrarian Democracy" at the close of the 19th century?

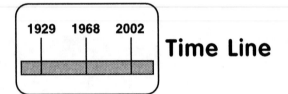

Time Line

Develop a time line listing events relevant to the following themes:

- The Grange Movement and Granger Laws

- Rise and Fall of the Populist or People's Party

- 19th-Century Farmers' Organizations

Decision-Making Scenarios

- If you were a delegate at the 1892 Populist or People's Party Convention, which plank would you have lobbied to remove from the Omaha Platform and what issue/position would you have replaced it with?

- If you were a leader in the Populist or People's Party in 1896 would you have supported the candidacy of the Democratic Party nominee, William Jennings Bryan, a pro-farmer politician, or selected another candidate to run on your party's ticket? Explain.

- If you were a farmer in the late 19th century and realized that most of the profit from your crop went to the "middlemen" (e.g., grain-elevator operators, railroads), would you continue farming or migrate to the cities to find employment as many other farmers did during this period? Explain.

Farmer's Revolt *(cont.)*

 ## Concept Maps

Develop a concept map for each of the following:

- Farmers' Alliances
- The Grange
- Populists
- Rural Protest

 ## Venn Diagrams

Farmers' Attempts to Organize vs. Labor's Attempts to Organize: Compare and contrast the attempts by farmers and workers to organize during the 19th century.

Populist Party Successes & Failures vs. Grange Movement Successes & Failures: Compare and contrast the political and economic objectives, as well as the successes and failures of the Populist Party and the Grange Movement in the late 19th century.

 ## Vee Heuristics

Farmers' Declaration of Independence vs. Original Declaration of Independence: How did the 1873 Farmers' Declaration of Independence differ from the original, 1776 Declaration of Independence drafted by Thomas Jefferson?

Positive Impact of Agricultural Mechanization vs. Negative Impact of Agricultural Mechanization: How did the mechanization of American farmers during the 19th century have both a positive and negative impact on farmers?

New South and American West

Journal Prompts

- What impact did the stereotypical image of African Americans portrayed in the popular culture of the late 19th century have on race relations in the United States?

- Why is Joseph Gliden's invention of barbed wire in 1874 seen by some as a major turning point in the history of the American West? What other events do you believe played a role in transforming the West during the late 19th century?

- How did Native Americans and the U.S. military and government leaders differ in their view of the events that occurred at Little Big Horn River in present-day Montana in 1876?

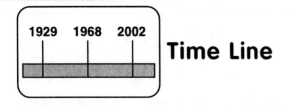

Time Line

Develop a time line listing events relevant to the following themes:

- Post-Reconstruction Disenfranchisement of African Americans in the South

- Late-19th-Century Transformation of the Southern Economy

- Indian Wars, 1860–1890

Decision-Making Scenarios

- If you worked for Henry Grady at the *Atlanta Constitution* during the late 19th century and were assigned to help him with the "New South" campaign, what changes would you recommend needed to be made in the South to bring them into the soon-to-be 20th century?

- If you were a young African-American "Buffalo Soldier" assigned to a U.S. Cavalry unit stationed in the West during the late 19th century, describe in a letter home your reaction to the treatment of Native Americans and what you felt should be done about it.

- If you were a newspaper editor in 1890 and just learned of the U.S. Census Department's announcement that for the first time in history there was no longer a definable "frontier line" in America, how would your editorial column read the next day?

New South and American West *(cont.)*

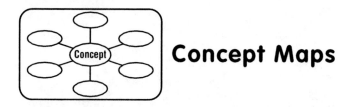 ## Concept Maps

Develop a concept map for each of the following:

- American Bison or Buffalo
- Jim Crow Laws
- "New South"
- Wounded Knee

 ## Venn Diagrams

Antebellum South vs. "New South": Compare and contrast the antebellum South with the "New South" of the post-Civil War period.

Native Americans in the Indian Wars vs. U.S. Military in the Indian Wars: Compare and contrast the advantages and disadvantages as well as the victories and defeats of the Native Americans and U.S. military during the Indian Wars of the late 19th century.

 ## Vee Heuristics

Status of African Americans in the "New South" vs. Status of African Americans during Reconstruction: How did life for African Americans in the "New South" differ from that of the Reconstruction period?

"First Great Removal" vs. "Second Great Removal": How did the "Second Great Removal" of Native Americans in the late 19th century differ from the "First Great Removal," which occurred during the first half of the 19th century?

Industrial America

Journal Prompts

- How did the government support the industrial growth America experienced during the late 19th century? Was government intervention or lack of intervention the key to America's economic success during this period?

- What is the meaning of the following Thomas Edison quote: "Genius is one percent inspiration and ninety-nine percent perspiration"? Was he correct? Explain.

- Was William Vanderbilt's observation concerning American industry accurate when he stated in 1882 that "railroads are not run for the benefit of the dear public . . . they are built for the men who invest their money and expect to [make a] profit"? Explain.

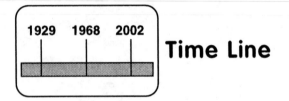

Time Line

Develop a time line listing events relevant to the following themes:

- Inventions and Inventors

- Rise of American Businesses and Trusts

- Late-19th- and Early-20th-Century Philanthropy

Decision-Making Scenarios

- If you were a young assistant to Thomas Edison at his Menlo Park lab and he asked you what he should invent next to help prepare America for the 20th century, what would you suggest and why?

- If you were a member of Congress who had just discovered that the railroad companies had been granted over 150 million acres of public land and that one third of the money invested to build the nation's railroads was from foreign investors, what would you do?

- If you lived in a late-19th-century city in which your family and friends were dependent upon the local industrial plants, what would you do if you discovered that these factories were polluting the air and water supply for your community?

Industrial America *(cont.)*

Concept Maps

Develop a concept map for each of the following:

- "Gospel of Wealth"

- *Laissez Faire*

- Robber Barons

- Trusts

Venn Diagrams

Horizontal Integration vs. Vertical Integration: Compare and contrast the basic economic organization and rationale for the late-19th-century business practices known as horizontal and vertical integration.

19th-Century Industrialists vs. 21st-Century Entrepreneurs: Compare and contrast the business practices and public perception of 19th-century industrialists (e.g., John D. Rockefeller) with those of present-day entrepreneurs (e.g., Bill Gates).

Vee Heuristics

Intent of the Sherman Anti-Trust Act vs. Implementation of the Sherman Anti-Trust Act: How did the original intent of the Sherman Anti-trust Act drastically differ from what occurred when it was implemented in 1890?

Industrialist Legacy vs. Philanthropist Legacy: How did the legacy of wealthy 19th century robber barons, such as Cornelius Vanderbilt, as businessmen and industrialists differ from their legacy as philanthropists?

Immigration and American Cities

Journal Prompts

- Was the urbanization of America inevitable or did certain factors in the 19th century set the nation on that course? Explain.

- Why was there an increase in African-American migration to American Urban areas during the late 19th century?

- Has America always honored the premise of the Emma Lazarus penned inscription on the base of the Statue of Liberty, "Give me your tired, your poor, your huddled masses yearning to breathe free"? Explain.

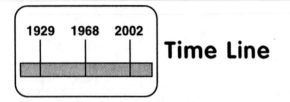

Time Line

Develop a time line listing events relevant to the following themes:

- Late 19th Century Immigration
- 19th Century Nativist Organizations and Activities
- 19th Century Urban Growth

Decision-Making Scenarios

- If you were a new immigrant to the United States in the late 19th century, what would you write your friends back home about your new home in America?

- If you were a member of Congress during the late 19th century when a proposed bill requiring literacy tests for immigrants was being debated, what would you say when it came time to voice your opinion on the floor of the House?

- If you were the mayor of a 19th-century city and could only fund three initiatives designed to address the many problems facing the people in your community, what efforts would you choose to fund and why?

Immigration and American Cities *(cont.)*

 ## Concept Maps

Develop a concept map for each of the following:

- Immigration
- Segregation
- Success Ethic
- Urbanization

 ## Venn Diagrams

Melting Pot vs. Cultural Mosaic: Compare and contrast the meaning of the labels or phrases used in American history textbooks during the 20th century to describe American society.

New Immigration vs. Old Immigration: Compare and contrast the different ethnic and cultural groups that came to the United States, as well as their motivation for coming to America and the treatment they received upon arrival during the late 19th century with those of earlier waves of immigrants.

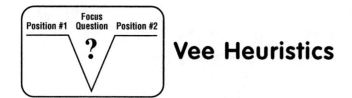 ## Vee Heuristics

Booker T. Washington's "Atlanta Compromise" vs. W.E.B. Du Bois' "Talented Tenth": How did Booker T. Washington and W.E.B. Du Bois differ in their view of how African Americans should attempt to gain equal rights?

Upper Class View of "Rags to Riches" Thesis vs. Lower Class View of "Rags to Riches" Thesis: How did wealthy and poor Americans differ in their interpretation of late-19th-century Horatio Alger "rags to riches" novels?

Rise of Labor Unions

Journal Prompts

- Why did it take so long for the government to recognize the right of workers to organize and be members of labor unions?

- What is the meaning of the following quote by AFL President Samuel Gompers: "Show me the country in which there are no strikes and I'll show you that country in which there is no liberty"? Is his observation accurate or is it an exaggeration? Explain.

- Why do you believe Labor Day was officially declared a national holiday in 1894? Does it have the same meaning today as it did over a century ago?

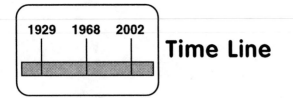

Time Line

Develop a time line listing events relevant to the following themes:

- Rise of 19th-Century Labor Unions

- 19th-Century Strikes

- 19th-Century Labor Legislation and Court Decisions

Decision-Making Scenarios

- If you were an experienced female factory worker in the 19th century making $5 a week, what would you do if you found out that newly-hired, unskilled male workers in your factory were earning $8 a week?

- If you were told by your parent that you had to go to work in a factory at the age of ten in order for your family to pay their bills, what would your diary entry read after your first day of work?

- If you were one of the workers who participated in the Pullman Strike of 1894 and witnessed the use of federal troops to crush the strikers, resulting in the death of many of your fellow workers, would this make you more committed to the American Railway Union cause or doubtful about their chance to bring about change? Explain.

Rise of Labor Unions *(cont.)*

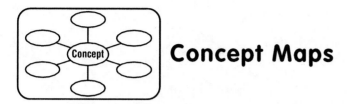

Concept Maps

Develop a concept map for each of the following:

- 8-Hour Workday
- Child Labor
- Strikes
- Unions

Venn Diagrams

American Federation of Labor vs. National Labor Union & Knights of Labor: Compare and contrast the goals and tactics, as well as the successes and failures of the American Federation of Labor with those of its two 19th-century predecessors, the National Labor Union and Knights of Labor.

19th-Century Labor Unions vs. 21st-Century Labor Unions: Compare and contrast the role labor unions played in the late 19th century with the role they play today.

Vee Heuristics

Female Workers' Experiences vs. White Male Workers' Experiences: How did the experiences of female workers differ from that of their white male counterparts during the 19th century?

Workers' View of Homestead Strike vs. Industrialists & Government's View of Homestead Strike: How did workers' view of the Homestead Strike of 1892 differ from that of wealthy industrialists and government officials?

The Gilded Age

Journal Prompts

• If so many Gilded Age politicians were viewed as either corrupt or inept, why was voter turnout during this period higher than it has been elsewhere in American history?

• Would James Blaine have lost the presidential election of 1884 if he hadn't given what has been termed the "3Rs Speech," in which he made a slanderous remark concerning Catholic and Irish voters? Explain. Do you think one remark in a speech could ruin a candidate's chances for victory today? Explain.

• Would civil-service reform have been implemented if not for the assassination of President James Garfield? Explain. What are other examples of political changes that have occurred in American history as a result of tragic events?

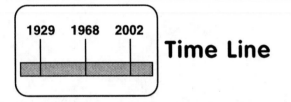

Time Line

Develop a time line listing events relevant to the following themes:

• Gilded Age Presidential Elections

• Gilded Age Legislation

• Gilded Age Scandals and Corruption

Decision-Making Scenarios

• If you were a member of Congress during the Gilded Age, a period in which two presidential candidates won the popular vote only to lose the electoral college, would you vote for a bill calling for an end to the electoral college system? Explain.

• If you were a voter in the 1884 election, would you have voted for a corrupt politician that was a good family man (James Blaine) or an honest politician with a colored past (Grover Cleveland)? Explain.

• If you were a political cartoonist during the Gilded Age, like Thomas Nast, would you have attacked the corruption of the period, knowing that one of the political leaders or robber barons you depicted in your cartoons may work to get you fired? Explain.

The Gilded Age *(cont.)*

 ## Concept Maps

Develop a concept map for each of the following:

- Gilded Age
- Gospel of Wealth
- Mugwumps
- Social Darwinism

 ## Venn Diagrams

Gilded Age Presidential Politics vs. Late 20th/Early 21st-Century Presidential Politics: Compare and contrast the Gilded Age presidential election campaign tactics, issues, voting turnout, and results with those of a century later.

Positive Actions of Big-City Bosses vs. Negative Actions of Big-City Bosses: Compare and contrast the positive and negative things big city political bosses like "Big Tim" Sullivan of New York City did for their constituents.

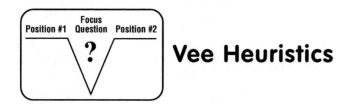 ## Vee Heuristics

Northern View of the Election of 1876 vs. Southern View of the Election of 1876: How did the North and South differ in their view of the results of the election of 1876?

General Ulysses S. Grant vs. President Ulysses S. Grant: How did Ulysses S. Grant's legacy as a Civil War general differ from that which emerged from this two terms as president during the Gilded Age?

Rise of the Middle Class and Consumer Culture

Journal Prompts

- Why did late-19th-century and early-20th-century Americans become so fascinated with sports (e.g., basketball was invented in 1891, the first World Series was played in 1901)?

- Why did so many Americans become involved with large-scale amusement activities during the turn of the century (e.g., the first amusement park was founded at Coney Island, Barnum and Bailey Circus was formed)?

- Why did late-19th-century Americans develop such a fondness for name-brand items such as Nabisco crackers, Tootsie Rolls, Campbell's soup, and Coca-Cola? Why has this name-brand loyalty remained to the present day?

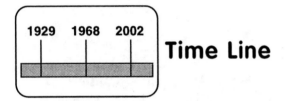

Time Line

Develop a time line listing events relevant to the following themes:

- Rise of Public Education in the 19th Century
- New Freedoms Gained by Women in the 19th Century
- Increased Role of Entertainment and Sports in American Society

Decision-Making Scenarios

- If you were a female college student during the late 19th century, how would you feel about the opportunity you had to get a college degree when you recognized that only 1 in 10 of your fellow students were female?

- If you attended a lecture by British social philosopher Herbert Spencer, who applied Darwin's theory to society and justified poverty in America by saying that the poor are not the "fittest" and therefore should not be helped, what would you do?

- If you were a member of the lower class during the late 19th century, what options did you have available to you that would allow you to climb the socio-economic ladder? Which of these options would you choose and why?

Rise of the Middle Class and Consumer Culture *(cont.)*

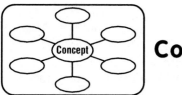 ## Concept Maps

Develop a concept map for each of the following:

- Consumer Culture
- Leisure
- Middle Class
- Social Mobility

 ## Venn Diagrams

Antebellum Socio-Economic Structure vs. Turn-of-the-Century Socio-Economic Structure:
Compare and contrast the social-economic structure in antebellum America with that of the late 19th century and early 20th century.

Early-19th-Century Education vs. Late-19th-Century and Early-20th-Century Education:
Compare and contrast the role education played in American society in the early 19th century with that of the late 19th century and early 20th century.

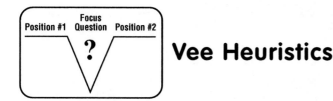 ## Vee Heuristics

Compulsory School Attendance Laws vs. Not Mandating School Attendance: Why did some states—31 by 1901—require school attendance until children reached a certain age, while other states weren't even considering passing such compulsory school-attendance laws?

Two Steps Forward for Women vs. One Step Back for Women: How did the new freedoms and benefits gained by women during the late 19th century reflect the old saying of "two steps forward, one step back"?

America Builds an Empire

Journal Prompts

- What role did the "closing of the frontier" (the American West) play in influencing American foreign policy during the late 19th century?

- How did the Americans and British differ in their view of what should be done to resolve the Venezuela-British Guiana boundary dispute of 1895? What was ironic about how the controversy ended?

- What did Teddy Roosevelt mean when he described his foreign policy approach as "Speak softly, but carry a big stick"? Would such an approach work today? Explain.

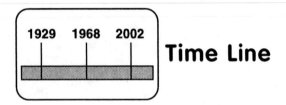

Time Line

Develop a time line listing events relevant to the following themes:
- American Territorial Expansion, 1865–1900
- American Foreign Policy, 1865–1900
- American Foreign Trade, 1865–1900

Decision-Making Scenarios

- If you were a newspaper journalist sent to Hawaii in 1893 to cover the "Hawaiian Revolution," what would you have reported in your article?

- If you were a member of the Senate during the time of the Panama Revolution, would you have voted to ratify the Panama Canal Treaty after you found out about the role of the U.S. Navy in assisting in overthrowing Colombian rule in Panama? Explain.

- Given Teddy Roosevelt's previous history, if you were a member of the Nobel Prize Committee, would you have voted to award him the 1906 Nobel Peace Prize for his role in bringing an end to the Russo-Japanese War? Explain.

America Builds an Empire (cont.)

 ## Concept Maps

Develop a concept map for each of the following:

- Annexation
- Imperialism
- New Manifest Destiny
- "New Outlook"

 ## Venn Diagrams

"New Outlook" Foreign Policy vs. "New Manifest Destiny" Foreign Policy: Compare and contrast the "New Outlook" American foreign policy approach of the 1880s with the "New Manifest Destiny" approach that was implemented in the 1890s.

Annexation of Alaska vs. Annexation of Hawaii: Compare and contrast how the United States acquired Alaska in 1867 with how it acquired Hawaii a generation later.

 ## Vee Heuristics

Manifest Destiny Territorial Acquisition vs. "New Manifest Destiny" Territorial Acquisition: How did the tactics used to gain territories during the first half of the 19th century, as part of Manifest Destiny, differ from those used to gain territories under the "New Manifest Destiny" policies of the late 19th century?

Roosevelt's Corollary to the Monroe Doctrine vs. Monroe Doctrine: How did "Roosevelt's Corollary of the Monroe Doctrine," authored by President Theodore Roosevelt, differ from the original Monroe Doctrine, penned by Secretary of State John Quincy Adams?

Spanish-American War

Journal Prompts

• How did the account of what occurred during the Cuban revolt that most Americans heard from the government and press differ from what actually took place starting in 1895?

• How did the role of the War Hawks in the War of 1812 differ from the role played by the Yellow Press in the Spanish-American War?

• What "lessons" did America learn from the Spanish-American War? Did the nation ever make the same mistakes in the five wars it engaged in during the next century? Explain.

1929 1968 2002 Time Line

Develop a time line listing events relevant to the following themes:

• Cuban Revolt

• Spanish-American War

• Filipino Insurrection

Decision-Making Scenarios

• If you were a young person who joined the military to fight to "free Cuba from Spanish rule" during the Spanish-American War, how would you react if you were informed that you were being transferred to the Philippines to put down a rebellion by Filipinos protesting American rule?

• Why did future Secretary of State John Hay say that he thought the Spanish-American War was "a splendid little war"? Should any war ever be referred to as this? Explain.

• If you were a member of the Anti-Imperialist League and wanted to convince your friends and colleagues that the annexation of the Philippines was wrong, what would you tell them that might convince them that your position on this issue is correct?

Spanish-American War *(cont.)*

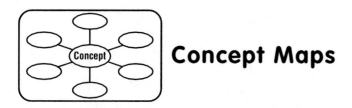

Concept Maps

Develop a concept map for each of the following:

- "Remember the Maine"

- Rough Riders

- "Splendid Little War"

- Yellow Journalism

Venn Diagrams

Spanish Advantages vs. American Advantages: Compare and contrast the advantages held by the Spanish and Americans in the Spanish-American War.

Spanish Disadvantages vs. American Disadvantages: Compare and contrast the disadvantages or obstacles that the Spanish and Americans faced in the Spanish-American War.

Vee Heuristics

Spanish Interpretation of the *U.S.S. Maine* Incident vs. American Interpretation of the *U.S.S. Maine* Incident: How did the Spanish government's interpretation of the sinking of the *U.S.S. Maine* differ from that of the United States government?

Emilio Aguinaldo during the Spanish-American War vs. Emilio Aguinaldo during the Filipino Insurrection: How did Americans' view of the role Emilio Aguinado played during the Spanish-American War differ from how they perceived of his role in the Filipino Insurrection?

Social Justice Movement

Journal Prompts

- What injustices did social reformers focus their attention and efforts on during the late 19th/early 20th century? Who did they blame for these societal ills?

- If social justice and progressive movement leaders hadn't shed light on the problems that plagued American cities during the late 19th/early 20th century, what would have happened? Would these problems have ever been addressed and if so how?

- Why did it take so long for women to gain the right to vote in America? Could it have occurred earlier? Explain.

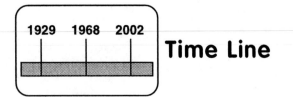

Time Line

Develop a time line listing events relevant to the following themes:

- Rise of the Socialist Party
- Late 19th/Early 20th Century Social Reforms
- Women's Suffrage Movement

Decision-Making Scenarios

- If you were a recent immigrant to the United States during the early 20th century and found yourself five years later still living in a disease-ridden tenement house, unable to ever save enough money to climb the social ladder, would you remain in America or attempt to return home? Explain.

- If you were a member of a middle-class family living in a nice home and enjoying a high standard of living, would you become active in the social justice movement? Explain.

- If you were one of the 27 million visitors to the 1893 Chicago World's Colombian Exposition and saw all of the "stupendous results of American enterprise" such as the latest inventions and other modern mechanical accomplishments, only to go back that night and find children living in the filthy streets just a few blocks away from your hotel, begging for money, what would you think? Would you be moved to take action? Explain why or why not.

Social Justice Movement *(cont.)*

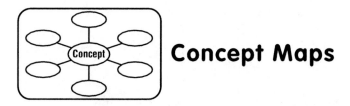 ## Concept Maps

Develop a concept map for each of the following:

- Australian Ballot
- Justice
- Socialists
- Suffrage

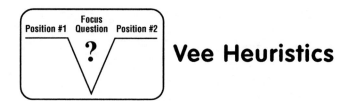 ## Venn Diagrams

Social Justice Movement vs. Civil Rights Movement: Compare and contrast the activities of the social justice movement of the early 20th century with the civil rights movement a half-century later.

Positive Motives of Social Justice Activists vs. Negative Motives of Social Justice Activists: Compare and contrast the positive and negative motives that prompted many middle class Americans to become social justice activists during the late 19th/early 20th century.

 ## Vee Heuristics

Triangle Fire as Tragedy vs. Triangle Fire as a Positive Catalyst: How could both good and bad result from the Triangle Shirtwaist Company Fire of 1911?

Western States' View of Women's Rights vs. Eastern States' View of Women's Rights: How did residents in states west of the Mississippi River differ from those east of the mighty river in their view of women's political rights during the late 19th/early 20th century?

The Progressive Era

Journal Prompts

- Are books such as Upton Sinclair's *The Jungle* as effective today in bringing about social change as they were during the Progressive Era, or has television and film become a more effective way to move Americans to action?

- Was the Progressive-Era reformers' victory in getting the 18ᵗʰ Amendment (Prohibition) passed a real victory or defeat? Explain.

- Was Teddy Roosevelt correct when he characterized the writers of the Progressive Era who uncovered one scandal or societal problem after another as "muckrakers," people who just stir up or shovel "muck" all day but really don't contribute much, if anything, to the solution? Explain.

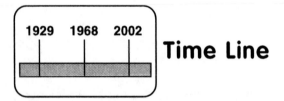

Time Line

Develop a time line listing events relevant to the following themes:
- Progressive Era Legislative Reforms
- Progressive Era Supreme Court Decisions
- Publication of Muckraking Articles and Books

Decision-Making Scenarios

- If you were Secretary of Agriculture during the Progressive Era, would you have put a stop to Chief Chemist Dr. H.W. Wiley's "poison squad" testing of medicines on his "human guinea pig" assistants in an attempt to see if they were safe for children and adults? Explain.

- If you were a young journalist during the Progressive Era, on what issue or problem would you focus your writing? What would you hope to accomplish with the publication of your article or book?

- What would you do if you were living in the Progressive Era and had just read a newspaper article or book depicting the tragic story of children your age that were forced to work in the mines or factories that dotted the American landscape at that time?

The Progressive Era *(cont.)*

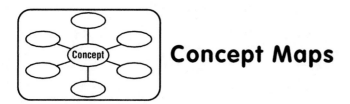

Concept Maps

Develop a concept map for each of the following:

- Muckraker

- Progressivism

- Pure Food and Drug Act

- "Wisconsin Idea"

Venn Diagrams

TR's Progressive Reforms vs. Taft's Progressive Reforms: Compare and contrast the progressive reforms implemented by Presidents Theodore Roosevelt and William Howard Taft.

Women's Role in the Progressive Movement vs. African Americans' Role in the Progressive Movement: Compare and contrast the goals, tactics, successes and setbacks experienced by women and African-American reformers during the Progressive Era.

Vee Heuristics

Investigative Journalists' Methodology vs. Muckrakers' Methodology: How do the methods of investigative television and print journalists today differ from those used by the muckrakers nearly a century ago?

Radical Progressivism vs. Moderate Progressivism: How did the radical and more moderate leaders of the progressive movement differ in how they thought the problems they had exposed should be dealt with?

The TR, Taft, and Wilson Years

Journal Prompts

- Is Teddy Roosevelt as deserving as Washington, Jefferson, and Lincoln to have his image immortalized on Mount Rushmore? If you agree, explain why. If you disagree, discuss who you think is more deserving.

- If you were William Howard Taft and had no interest in becoming president, would you still accept the offer to run for the office if Teddy Roosevelt personally asked you and you knew you would win? Explain.

- Woodrow Wilson is the only person ever to serve as president of the United States who also had a Ph.D. Is the candidate's education an important consideration when deciding who to vote for president or are there other factors that are more important? Explain.

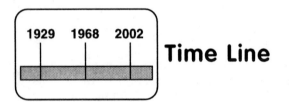

Time Line

Develop a time line listing events relevant to the following themes:

- 20th-Century Environmental Movement
- Progressive-Era Presidential Elections
- Niagara Movement

Decision-Making Scenarios

- If you were a young voter during the 1912 presidential election, who would you vote for (TR, Taft, Wilson, or Debs) and why?

- If you were an advisor to President Theodore Roosevelt and he asked you what you thought about his proposal to ban the White House Christmas tree (which he did in 1902) as an example of conservationism, what would you tell him?

- If you were an advisor to President Woodrow Wilson when he suffered a stroke in 1919 and was incapable of running the government for the next year, would you have encouraged him to step down or to continue to manage the affairs of state from his bed with his wife acting as a liaison? Explain.

The TR, Taft, and Wilson Years *(cont.)*

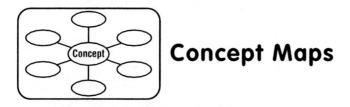 ## Concept Maps

Develop a concept map for each of the following:

- "Bully Pulpit"
- "New Nationalism"
- "Dollar Diplomacy"
- Trustbuster

 ## Venn Diagrams

Roosevelt Administration vs. Taft Administration: Compare and contrast the conservation/environmental and trustbusting accomplishments of the Theodore Roosevelt and William Howard Taft administrations.

TR's "Square Deal" vs. Wilson's "New Freedom": Compare and contrast President Theodore Roosevelt's domestic program for Americans, which was called the "Square Deal," with the domestic program President Woodrow Wilson outlined nearly a decade later, which was labeled "New Freedom."

 ## Vee Heuristics

TR's View of the Ballinger-Pinchot Controversy vs. Taft's View of the Ballinger-Pinchot Controversy: How did Theodore Roosevelt and William Howard Taft differ in their view of the controversy surrounding the rift between Secretary of the Interior Richard Ballinger and Chief U.S. Forester Gifford Pinchot?

President Taft's Accomplishments vs. Chief Justice Taft's Accomplishments: How did William Howard Taft's accomplishments as president of the United States differ from his accomplishments as chief justice of the Supreme Court?

World War I: European Battlefield

Journal Prompts

- Did President Wilson's claim that World War I was the "war to end all wars" and a "war to make the world safe for democracy" help or hurt the war effort and legacy of the war in the coming decade? Explain.

- After World War I was over, why did no one refer to it as a "splendid little war," as Secretary of State John Hay did following the Spanish-American War?

- During World War I, recruits and draftees were required to take a series of physical and mental tests, in which it was found that 31 percent of them were illiterate and 29 percent were physically unfit for service. If you were President Wilson, what would you do about these shocking findings?

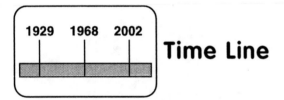

Time Line

Develop a time line listing events relevant to the following themes:

- European Events that Led to the Outbreak of World War I in 1914
- World War I (1914–1917)
- American Involvement in World War I (1917–1918)

Decision-Making Scenarios

- If you were one of the American doughboys who fought in the trenches of Europe during World War I, what would you tell your family back home in a letter about what you had experienced and what you thought of the war?

- If you were one of the women who went to work in the factories or shipyards during World War I, what would you do when you were told to go home once the war was over?

- If you were a young African American who was drafted into the military during World War I, how would you respond to the fact that you were fighting to "restore democracy and freedom" in Europe while you were serving in a segregated U.S. Army and lived in a nation that denied you many freedoms?

World War I: European Battlefield *(cont.)*

Concept Maps

Develop a concept map for each of the following:

- AEF
- Fourteen Points
- Neutrality
- Trench Warfare

Venn Diagrams

World War I Warfare vs. 19ᵗʰ-Century Warfare: Compare and contrast the type of warfare Americans experienced during World War I with that of 19ᵗʰ-century conflicts in which the U.S. military was involved.

Fourteen Points as a Realistic Post-War Vision of the World vs. Fourteen Points as an Idealistic Post-War vision of the World: Compare and contrast the realistic or pragmatic features included in Woodrow Wilson's Fourteen Points with the more idealistic proposals outlined in the President's document.

Vee Heuristics

German View of Wilson's Neutrality Position vs. U.S. View of Wilson's Neutrality Position: How did Germany and the United States differ in how they viewed President Wilson's official policy of neutrality in World War I from 1914–1917?

German Interpretation of the Sinking of the *Lusitania* vs. American Interpretation of the Sinking of the *Lusitania*: How did Germans and Americans differ in their view of who was to blame for the sinking of the *Lusitania* in 1915?

World War I: Home Front

Journal Prompts

- During World War I, why did President Wilson tell the Senate that voting in favor of women's suffrage was "vital to winning the war"?

- Why were there so many "draft dodgers"—over 300,000—during World War I? What should President Wilson have done with these individuals?

- What is the meaning of the following World War I era question: "How are you going to keep them [returning soldiers] down on the farm once they've seen Paris?" Did this prediction come true? Explain.

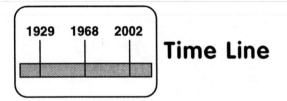

Time Line

Develop a time line listing events relevant to the following themes:

- World War I Programs and Administrations/Boards

- World War I Era Legislation and Supreme Court Rulings

- Increase in Military Preparedness, 1914–1918

Decision-Making Scenarios

- If you were an American of German ancestry during World War I, what would you do in response to all of the anti-German propaganda and actions you witnessed during this period?

- If you were one of the professors or teachers fired during World War I for questioning the morality of the war or the necessity of American involvement in the European conflict, what would you write in a letter to the editor of your local newspaper?

- If you were a member of the U.S. delegation at the Paris Peace Conference in 1918, what would you advise President Wilson should be removed from the proposed Treaty of Versailles, and what would you recommend be added?

World War I: Home Front *(cont.)*

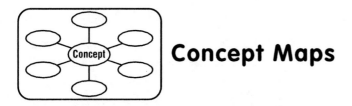

Concept Maps

Develop a concept map for each of the following:

- League of Nations
- Propaganda
- Selective Service
- Treaty of Versailles

Venn Diagrams

Positive View of the CPI vs. Negative View of the CPI: Compare and contrast the positive and negative features and legacy of the Committee on Public Information (CPI) or "Creel Committee."

American Economy & Society During World War I vs. American Economy & Society During 19ᵗʰ-Century Wars: Compare and contrast the impact of World War I on the American economy and society with that of the 19th-century wars the U.S. was involved in.

Vee Heuristics

World War I Era Espionage & Sedition Acts vs. Late 18ᵗʰ Century Alien & Sedition Acts: How did the intent and impact of the World War I era Espionage and Sedition Acts differ from that of the Alien and Sedition Acts that were passed by Congress during John Adams' Administration in the late 18th century?

President Wilson's View of the League of Nations vs. Republican Senators' View of the League of Nations: How did President Wilson and Republican leaders in the Senate differ in their evaluation of America's proposed role in the League of Nations?

Roaring Twenties

Journal Prompts

- What impact did radio and the telephone have on American society during the 1920s? How does this compare with the impact computers have had on American society during the late 20ᵗʰ century?

- Why did movie theaters average nearly 100 million moviegoers per week during the 1920s? Why do fewer people attend movies today than did over three-quarters of a century ago?

- Why were so many Americans fascinated with Charles Lindbergh becoming the first person to fly solo across the Atlantic Ocean in 1927? Why are Americans still just as infatuated with such record-breaking feats?

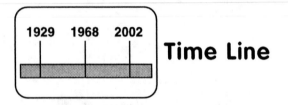

Time Line

Develop a time line listing events relevant to the following themes:

- Early-20ᵗʰ-Century Second Industrial Revolution
- The Prohibition Experiment
- 1920s Entertainment

Decision-Making Scenarios

- If you were a newspaper editor during the 1920s, what would you write in your editorial column about the recently released census report indicating that for the first time in American history the majority of Americans now lived in urban areas?

- Would you have bought a Model T or went to work for Ford Automotive during the 1920s if you found out that Henry Ford repeatedly wrote anti-Semitic articles in a Michigan newspaper? Explain.

- If you were a member of Congress during the 1920s, what would you have said during the floor debate on the proposed restrictive immigration laws that discriminated against individuals from Southern and Eastern Europe as well as Asia?

Roaring Twenties *(cont.)*

 **Concept Maps**

Develop a concept map for each of the following:

- Automobile
- Jazz Age
- Speakeasies
- "Talkies"

 **Venn Diagrams**

"Roaring Twenties" Image vs. 1920s Society Reality: Compare and contrast the image of the "Roaring Twenties" with the reality of how most Americans lived during the decade.

Positive Impact of the Automobile vs. Negative Impact of the Automobile: Compare and contrast the positive and negative impact the automobile had on the American landscape and society during the 1920s.

 **Vee Heuristics**

First Industrial Revolution vs. Second Industrial Revolution: How did the "first industrial revolution," which occurred during the 19th century, differ from the "second industrial revolution" of the early 20th century?

Progressive Era Middle-Class View of Alcohol vs. Prohibition-Era Middle-Class View of Alcohol: How did middle class reformers' portrayal of alcohol's negative impact on American society during the Progressive Era differ from their view of 1920s speakeasies that became popular during the Prohibition Era?

1920s: Anxiety and Red Scare

Journal Prompts

• What connection is there between the anti-German propaganda and actions witnessed during World War I and the record increase in membership of the Ku Klux Klan during the 1920s?

• Why did Americans become so fascinated with criminals (such as Al Capone) and crime (such as the St. Valentine's Day Massacre and the Lindbergh baby kidnapping) during the 1920s. Why has that interest with crime and criminals remained just as strong today?

• Was the "communist threat" in the United States during the 1920s as great as the government said it was? What is the legacy of the 1920s Red Scare?

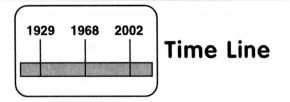

Time Line

Develop a time line listing events relevant to the following themes:

• Red Scare

• "Lost Generation" Literary Movement

• Harlem Renaissance Literary Movement

Decision-Making Scenarios

• If you were the jury foreman in the Sacco-Vanzetti Case of 1921, what verdict would you have supported and why?

• If you were a Harlem Renaissance or "Lost Generation" writer during the 1920s, what topic would you choose to write on and what would you hope the impact of your book would be?

• If you were one of the thousands of African Americans who lived in the South but migrated to the North during the 1920s to find employment in one of that region's cities, how would you react to the segregation you experienced in the workplace and neighborhood?

1920s: **Anxiety and Red Scare** *(cont.)*

 ## Concept Maps

Develop a concept map for each of the following:

- Harlem Renaissance
- "Lost Generation"
- Red Scare
- Scopes Monkey Trial

 ## Venn Diagrams

"Lost Generation" vs. Harlem Renaissance: Compare and contrast the literary style and contributions of "Lost Generation" and Harlem Renaissance authors.

Positive Impact of Marcus Garvey vs. Negative Impact of Marcus Garvey: Compare and contrast the positive and negative impact Marcus Garvey had on the black pride movement during the 1920s.

 ## Vee Heuristics

William Jennings Bryan's View of the Scopes Monkey Trial vs. Clarence Darrow's View of the Scopes Monkey Trial: How did William Jennings Bryan's and Clarence Darrow's interpretation of the arrest and trial of John Scopes in 1925 differ?

Flapper Image of Women vs. Victorian Image of Women: How did the flapper image of women in the 1920s differ from the view of women during the Victorian period?

The Great Depression

Journal Prompts

- What were the major causes of the Great Depression? Was this economic downturn inevitable? Explain.

- What does the following Depression-era song lyric attempt to portray: "Once I built a tower, to the sun./Now it's done, Brother can you spare a dime?"

- What might have happened to Louisiana politician Huey Long and his "Share Our Wealth" movement had he not been assassinated in 1935?

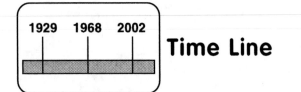

Time Line

Develop a time line listing events relevant to the following themes:

- Economic Decline Following the Stock Market Crash
- President Herbert Hoover's Initiatives
- Depression-Era Elections

Decision-Making Scenarios

- If you were an advisor for President Hoover, what actions would you recommend he take to alleviate the economic suffering that was going on in the nation?

- During the Great Depression, if you had a family to provide for and like millions of Americans found yourself out of work, what would you do? If that failed, what would you try next?

- If you were a reporter in 1932 covering the Bonus Army March in Washington, what would your column read like the day after the "Battle of Anacostia Flats"?

The Great Depression *(cont.)*

Concept Maps

Develop a concept map for each of the following:

- "Black Tuesday"
- Bonus Army
- Great Depression
- "Trickle Down"

Venn Diagrams

Impact of Great Depression vs. Impact of 19ᵗʰ-Century Economic Downturns: Compare and contrast the economic, political and social impact of the Great Depression on American society with that of previous economic downturns experienced during the 19ᵗʰ century.

Impact of Great Depression on Workers vs. Impact of Great Depression on Farmers: Compare and contrast the impact of the Great Depression on American workers and farmers.

Vee Heuristics

Herbert Hoover's World War I Public Image vs. Herbert Hoover's Depression-Era Public Image: How did Herbert Hoover's accomplishments and public image during World War I differ from his accomplishments and public image during the Great Depression?

Great Depression Impact on Men vs. Great Depression Impact on Women: How did the impact of the Great Depression on the economic, social, and psychological well being of men differ from the impact it had on women?

FDR's New Deal

Journal Prompts

- Was FDR justified in attempting to "pack" the Supreme Court by increasing the number of justices from 9 to 15? Explain.

- Was the nation correct in electing FDR to an unprecedented third term in 1940? Explain.

- The New Deal increased the national debt from $19 billion in 1932 to $40 billion in 1939. Was it worth the cost? Explain. Could it have been accomplished in a less expensive manner? Explain.

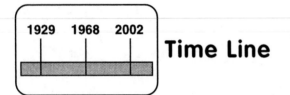

Time Line

Develop a time line listing events relevant to the following themes:

- President Roosevelt's First Hundred Days
- First New Deal
- Second New Deal

Decision-Making Scenarios

- If you were a member of the press corps during FDR's presidency and were told never to photograph President Roosevelt below the waist because of his paralysis, would you comply with the request? Explain.

- As a speechwriter for FDR assigned to compose the first "Fireside Chat" for your boss, what would you write?

- If you were a member of FDR's "Brain Trust," assigned to examine the New Deal programs to determine what segment of the economy or society was being overlooked and then develop a program to address that need, what would be your recommendation?

FDR's New Deal *(cont.)*

Concept Maps

Develop a concept map for each of the following:

- Forgotten Man
- Relief
- Recovery
- Reform

Venn Diagrams

Hoover's Rugged Individualism vs. Roosevelt's New Deal: Compare and contrast Herbert Hoover's "Rugged Individualism" approach to confronting the Great Depression with Franklin D. Roosevelt's "New Deal."

New Deal Critics on the Left vs. New Deal Critics on the Right: Compare and contrast the criticism of the New Deal voiced by both the left/liberals and the right/conservatives.

Vee Heuristics

Hamiltonian Belief in a Strong Central Government vs. Jeffersonian Belief in the Common Man: How did FDR's New Deal embody both Hamiltonian support for a strong central government as well as Jeffersonian concern for the "common man"?

New Deal Successes vs. New Deal Failures: Which New Deal programs survived the 20th century and which programs failed? What factors account for the success or failure of the programs you identified?

World War II: European and Pacific Theaters

Journal Prompts

- If the Japanese had not bombed Pearl Harbor, when would the United States have entered World War II?

- Was the U.S. government and media justified in suppressing release of the actual toll the war was having on American lives, 300,000 soldiers perished during WWII, and not printing photos of dead American soldiers in battle until 1943? Explain.

- If you were a newspaper journalist, what would you write on V-E day, and later, for V-J day?

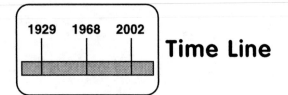

Time Line

Develop a time line listing events relevant to the following themes:

- Events that Led to the Outbreak of World War II
- World War II: European Theater
- World War II: Pacific Theater

Decision-Making Scenarios

- If you were a young American soldier who was in a unit that was to take part in Operation Overlord, what would you write the night before the D-Day invasion in a letter home to your family?

- If you were an African-American soldier and were subjected to segregated barracks, commissaries, military units, and if wounded in battle had to receive segregated blood, how would you feel? Would you do anything about these discriminatory practices? Explain.

- If you were an advisor to the president during World War II, what would you recommend be done in response to a War Department report estimating that the U.S. military strategy in the Pacific, known as "island hopping," would eventually cost one million American casualties before Japan would surrender?

World War II: European and Pacific Theaters *(cont.)*

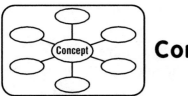

Concept Maps

Develop a concept map for each of the following:

- "Black Sunday"

- "Double V" Campaign

- Land-Lease

- V-E Day and V-J Day

Venn Diagrams

America's Entry into World War I vs. America's Entry into World War II: Compare and contrast the events that led America to break from its official policy of neutrality and enter World War I and World War II.

World War II Combat in the European Theater vs. World War II Combat in the Pacific Theater: Compare and contrast the type of combat, as well as the battlefield victories and losses American soldiers experienced in the European and Pacific theaters, during World War II.

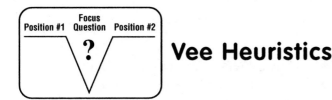

Vee Heuristics

America's Role & Contribution to World War I vs. America's Role & Contribution to World War II: How did America's role and contribution to the war effort during World War II differ from those of World War I?

Role of Women & African Americans in World War I vs. Role of Women & African Americans in World War II: How did the roles of women and African Americans in World War II differ from the roles they played in World War I?

World War II: Home Front

Journal Prompts

- Was American investment in the Manhattan Project worth the cost? What role did atomic weapons play in influencing events during World War II? How did this differ from the role atomic weapons would play in the coming decades?

- Was the compensation paid in 1988 to Japanese Americans who were interned during World War II justified? Are there other groups that should be compensated for similar events in American history? Explain.

- What role, if any, did wartime movies (such as *Letter from Bataan*) and songs (such as "Goodbye, Mamma, I'm Off to Yokohama") play in helping the American war effort during World War II?

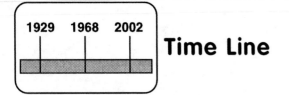

Time Line

Develop a time line listing events relevant to the following themes:

- Development of Atomic Weapons
- World War II Programs and Legislation
- Internment of Japanese Americans

Decision-Making Scenarios

- If you were one of the thousands of Japanese Americans who were removed from their homes and taken to an internment camp, how would you feel when you received notice from the U.S. government that your older brother, who had been drafted into the military, had been killed in battle?

- If you were one of the thousands of women who went to work in American factories during World War II (immortalized in the symbol of "Rosie the Riveter"), how might this experience shape your view of American society and your own goals for life?

- If you were placed in charge of the public-relations campaign for one of the eight war bond drives held during World War II, what strategy would you use to convince people to purchase these bonds?

World War II: Home Front *(cont.)*

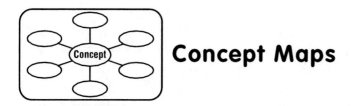 ## Concept Maps

Develop a concept map for each of the following:

- Executive Order 9066

- Manhattan Project

- Rationing

- "Rosie the Riveter"

 ## Venn Diagrams

World War II Preparedness & Mobilization vs. World War I Preparedness & Mobilization:
Compare and contrast American preparedness and mobilization efforts during World War II with those actions taken during World War I.

President Roosevelt's Leadership Style & Public Image vs. President Truman's Leadership Style & Public Image: Compare and contrast the presidential leadership styles and public image of Franklin D. Roosevelt and Harry S. Truman.

 ## Vee Heuristics

World War II Public Support vs. World War I Public Support: How did the challenge of convincing Americans to support the war effort and the efforts made by the government to build that public support during World War II differ from that of World War I?

Late-1940s View of Use of Atomic Weapons During World War II vs. Current View of Use of Atomic Weapons During World War II: How does the late-1940s view of President Harry S. Truman's use of atomic weapons against the Japanese at Hiroshima and Nagasaki during World War II differ from how it is viewed today in retrospect?

World War II: The Holocaust

Journal Prompts

- What lessons did Americans learn from the Holocaust? Could another Holocaust occur, or has one occurred since World War II? Explain.

- What impact did many of the Jewish refugees in the United States such as Albert Einstein and Edward Teller have on American society and history?

- Could the Holocaust have been prevented had other European nations not adopted a policy of appeasement during the 1930s and/or if the United States would have gotten involved in the European conflict prior to December 1941?

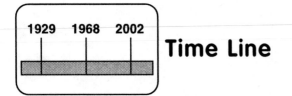

Time Line

Develop a time line listing events relevant to the following themes:

- Persecution and Extermination of European Jews under the Third Reich
- Attempts by Jewish Refugees to Flee Europe during the 1930s and '40s
- Nuremberg Trials

Decision-Making Scenarios

- If you were an African-American soldier during World War II whose unit helped to liberate one of the concentration camps in Europe, what would you have written to your family back home in American about your feelings at that time?

- If you were a member of the State Department during World War II, what would you do when you found out that your boss, Breckinridge Long, was determined to block approval for the *St. Louis*, a ship of Jewish refugees, to enter the United States?

- If you were one of the government officials who, as early as 1942, was privy to classified information concerning Nazi extermination of Jews, would you have released this information to the press if you realized that the government was not going to take any immediate action? Explain. If you did release this information, would this have made any difference? Explain.

World War II: The Holocaust *(cont.)*

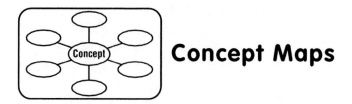

Concept Maps

Develop a concept map for each of the following:

- *Kristallnacht*
- Concentration Camps
- "Final Solution"
- Nuremberg Trials

Venn Diagrams

Persecution of Jews during Nazi Rule vs. Persecution of Native-American People during Spanish Conquest: Compare and contrast Nazi persecution of Jews in Europe during the 1930s and 1940s with the persecution of the indigenous people of the Americas at the hands of the conquistadors during the Spanish Conquest.

Holocaust = Horrible Actions by Bad People vs. Holocaust = Lack of Action by Good People: Compare and contrast the causes of the Holocaust as being attributed both to the horrible actions on the part of bad people as well as the lack of action on the part of good people.

Vee Heuristics

U.S. Government Policy on Refugees & Bombing vs. American Jewish Lobby Position on Refugees & Bombing: How did the U.S. State and War Departments' official positions on entry of Jewish refugees into the United States and the bombing of concentration camp gas chambers differ from that of American-Jewish lobbyists?

Discrimination Against African Americans & Japanese Americans in the United States during World War II vs. Discrimination Against Jews in Nazi Germany during the 1930s: How did the discrimination against African Americans and Japanese Americans in the United States during World War II differ from the discrimination against Jews in Nazi Germany during the 1930s?

Post-World War II Period

Journal Prompts

- How would post-World War II events have been different had Franklin D. Roosevelt lived to complete his fourth term?

- How were the problems facing Europe in the aftermath of World War II similar to those Americans faced during Reconstruction?

- Was National Security Council paper NSC-68—which was issued in 1950 and predicted a polarized world—a self-fulfilling prophecy? Explain.

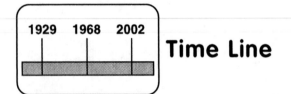

Time Line

Develop a time line listing events relevant to the following themes:

- Post-World War II European Aid Programs
- Establishment of the United Nations
- Post-World War II Demobilization and G.I. Programs

Decision-Making Scenarios

- If you were a returning soldier from World War II and were able to be the first in your family to attend college due to the G.I. Bill, how would you feel on graduation day?

- If you were an advisor to President Truman during the post-World War II period, what would you tell him would be another option to restore stability to Europe besides dividing the continent into zones or spheres of influence?

- If you were one of the American pilots who flew a total of 272,000 flights over West Berlin during the Soviet blockade in 1948–1949, what would you write your family back home concerning your experiences and how you felt about the entire mission?

Post-World War II Period *(cont.)*

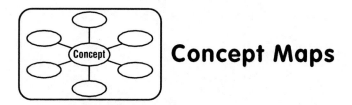

Concept Maps

Develop a concept map for each of the following:

- G.I. Bill
- Iron Curtain
- Marshall Plan
- United Nations

Venn Diagrams

Soldiers Return from World War II vs. Soldiers Return from Previous Wars: Compare and contrast the public reception and experiences of soldiers upon their return from World War II with that of previous 19th- and 20th-century wars.

Post-World War II United Nations vs. Post-World War I League of Nations: Compare and contrast the establishment, membership, goals, and objectives of the post-World War II United Nations with that of the post-World War I League of Nations.

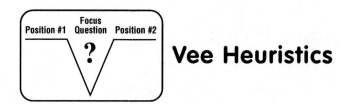

Vee Heuristics

FDR's Relationship with the Soviet Union vs. Truman's Relationship with the Soviet Union: How did President Harry S. Truman's relationship with the Soviet Union differ from that of former President Franklin D. Roosevelt?

Soldiers Return from World War II vs. Soldiers Return from Future Wars: How did the public reception and experiences of soldiers upon their return from World War II differ from that of those 20th-century wars that would follow?

Second Red Scare

Journal Prompts

- If you were a 1950s movie critic, what would you write about the anti-communist films of the period such as *I Married a Communist* and *Red Menace*?

- How was the Second Red Scare of the 1950s like the Salem Witchcraft hysteria of the 1690s?

- Why did it take so long for the nation to stand up to Senator Joseph McCarthy? What lesson did we learn from the Second Red Scare?

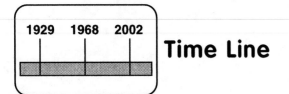

Time Line

Develop a time line listing events relevant to the following themes:

- Second Red Scare

- Rise and Fall of Senator Joseph McCarthy

- Red Scare Era Legislation and Judicial Rulings

Decision-Making Scenarios

- If you were called before the House Committee on Un-American Activities in the 1950s to testify about your friendship with suspected communists, would you provide the names of those individuals or remain silent? Explain.

- If you were an advisor to President Truman in 1950, when Senator Joseph McCarthy made his February 9th Lincoln Day claim of 200 communists being in the State Department, what would you recommend to the president that he do?

- If you were a member of Congress debating the 1952 McCarran-Walters Immigration Bill that would not allow immigrants into the United States if they held certain political beliefs, what would you say when it came your turn to speak?

Second Red Scare *(cont.)*

Concept Maps

Develop a concept map for each of the following:

- Blacklisting
- "Hollywood Ten"
- Rosenberg Trial
- Second Red Scare

Venn Diagrams

First Red Scare vs. Second Red Scare: Compare and contrast the causes and consequences of the First and Second Red Scare.

Palmer & Hoover's Role in First Red Scare vs. McCarthy & Nixon's Role in Second Red Scare: Compare and contrast the role and tactics used by A. Mitchell Palmer and J. Edgar Hoover in the First Red Scare with that of Joseph McCarthy and Richard Nixon in the Second Red Scare

Vee Heuristics

American View of Rosenberg's Trial vs. European View of Rosenberg's Trial: How did Americans and Europeans differ in their view of the Julius and Ethel Rosenberg arrest, trial, and execution during the 1950s?

McCarthy & HUAC's Portrayal of the "Communist Threat" vs. Actual Presence of Communists in American Society: How did the "communist threat" as portrayed by Senator Joseph McCarthy and the House Committee on Un-American Activities (HUAC) differ from the actual communist presence in American government, labor unions, and film industry during the late 1940s and 1950s?

Origins of the Cold War

Journal Prompts

- How would you feel if you were a student in 1957 and just found out from television that the Soviet Union had launched the first man-made satellite, *Sputnik,* into orbit?

- Was the CIA justified in supporting the overthrow of some Communist-leaning governments in Latin America (such as in Guatemala in 1954) during the 1950s? Explain.

- Should President Eisenhower have apologized to the Soviet Union, as Khrushchev demanded, for spying on them when the Soviets downed American pilot Francis Gary Powers' U-2 spy plane in 1960? Explain.

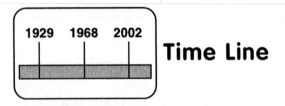

Time Line

Develop a time line listing events relevant to the following themes:

- Post-World War II Division of Europe

- Heightened Cold-War Tensions Between the U.S. and U.S.S.R.

- Cold-War Era Legislation and Programs

Decision-Making Scenarios

- If your family were considering purchasing a bomb shelter during the 1950s, what would you tell your parents if they asked for your opinion?

- If you were a newspaper reporter during the Cold War, what would you write in an article for your local paper when it was confirmed that the Soviet Union had successfully detonated their first atomic bomb?

- If you were a student during the 1950s and had just experienced your first "drop and cover" drill at school, how would you feel? What would you tell your parents when you got home that day?

Origins of the Cold War *(cont.)*

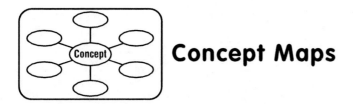

Concept Maps

Develop a concept map for each of the following:

- A-Bomb
- Containment
- NATO
- NSC-68

Venn Diagrams

North Atlantic Treaty Organization vs. Warsaw Pact: Compare and contrast the events that led to the establishment of North Atlantic Treaty Organization (NATO) and the Warsaw Pact, as well as the member nations, goals, successes, and setbacks experienced by each organization.

Positive View of the Division of Germany & Berlin vs. Negative View of the Division of Germany: Compare and contrast the positive and negative impact and legacy that resulted from the political division of Germany and Berlin in the late 1940s.

Vee Heuristics

U.S. View of the Chinese Revolution vs. U.S.S.R. View of the Chinese Revolution: How did the United States and Soviet Union differ in their view of the Mao Zedong-led Chinese Revolution of 1949?

American View of Truman Doctrine & Marshall Plan vs. Soviet View of Truman Doctrine & Marshall Plan: How did Americans and Soviets differ in their views of the Truman Doctrine and Marshall Plan of 1947?

Korean War

Journal Prompts

- Why did it take two of the three years America was involved in the Korean War to work out an armistice with the North Koreans after the stalemate at the 38th parallel in 1951?

- After he was relieved of command in the Korean War and was honored in a celebration attended by seven million people in New York City, why did General Douglas MacArthur seem to just "fade away"?

- Why is the Korean War known as the "forgotten war"?

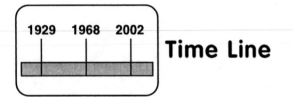

Time Line

Develop a time line listing events relevant to the following themes:

- Events that Led to the Start of the Korean War
- Korean War, 1950–1953
- Korean War Diplomatic Stalemate, 1951–1953

Decision-Making Scenarios

- If you were an African-American soldier during the Korean War, the first war in which black and white soldiers fought side-by-side in totally integrated units, what would you write in a letter to your father, who fought in World War II, and grandfather, who fought in World War I?

- If you were an advisor to President Truman during the Korean War, what would you recommend when he asked you if American military forces should cross the 38th parallel into North Korea after UN forces had already retaken South Korea from the North Korean invaders in October 1950? Explain.

- If you were a soldier who had returned home at the end of the war and was asked by your little brother and sister what you were fighting for in Korea, what would you tell them?

Korean War *(cont.)*

 ## Concept Maps

Develop a concept map for each of the following:

- Armistice
- Police Action
- Prisoner of War (POW)
- Stalemate

 ## Venn Diagrams

General MacArthur's Approach to Fighting the Korean War vs. President Truman's Approach to Fighting the Korean War: Compare and contrast General Douglas MacArthur and President Harry Truman's approach to fighting the Korean War.

Harry S. Truman's Presidential Style & Leadership vs. Dwight D. Eisenhower's Presidential Style & Leadership: Compare and contrast the presidential style of Presidents Harry S. Truman and Dwight D. Eisenhower, as well as their leadership in addressing the issues surrounding the war in Korea.

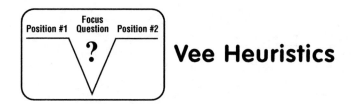 ## Vee Heuristics

American View of the Causes of the Korean War vs. Soviet View of the Causes of the Korean War: How did America and the Soviet Union differ in their views of the causes of the Korean War?

Legacy of Korean Conflict vs. Legacy of Previous Wars: How did the legacy of the Korean "conflict," which was a United Nations "police action" and undeclared war, differ from the legacy of previous "wars" in which Congress passed an official declaration of war?

1950s: Consensus and Conformity

Journal Prompts

- Was Secretary of Defense Charles Wilson, the former head of General Motors, correct when he said in the 1950s that "What's good for General Motors business is good for America"? Explain.

- What did sociologist David Riesman mean in his 1950 book *The Lonely Crowd* when he said that America was now a nation of "other directed" people, rather than "inner directed" people of the pre-World War II period? Was he correct? Explain.

- In 1900, one in eight teenagers was in school, but by 1950 that number had increased to six out of eight. What impact did this change have on American society?

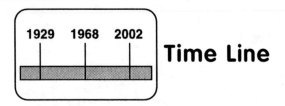

Time Line

Develop a time line listing events relevant to the following themes:

- Impact of the Post-World War II Baby Boom
- Growth of American Suburbs
- Rise of American Corporations

Decision-Making Scenarios

- If you were a young student during the 1950s and had the opportunity to attend the opening of the first McDonald's franchise in your community, how would you describe your experience to your friends the next day at school?

- If you were a teenager in 1950 and went with your parents to see films such as *Rebel Without a Cause* starring James Dean and *The Wild One* with Marlon Brando, what would you think after watching these movies? What do you think your parents might think?

- If you were a teenager in the 1950s, would you have listened to rock 'n' roll music? Explain why or why not. Why did some parents in the 1950s not want their children listening to such music?

1950s: Consensus and Conformity *(cont.)*

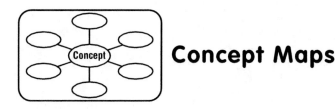

Concept Maps

Develop a concept map for each of the following:

- Baby Boom
- "I Like Ike"
- McDonald's Hamburger Stands
- Suburbs

Venn Diagrams

Depiction of American Family & Society in 1950s vs. Depiction of American Family & Society Today: Compare and contrast the depiction of the American family and society on television in the 1950s with that of today.

World War II Role & Image of Women vs. 1950s Role & Image of Women: Compare and contrast the role and image of women in American society during World War II with their role and image during the 1950s.

Vee Heuristics

Positive Effect of Suburbia vs. Negative Effect of Suburbia: How did the growth of suburbs during the 1950s have both a positive and negative effect on American society during the 1950s?

Positive Impact of the Interstate Highway Act vs. Negative Impact of the Interstate Highway Act: How did the Interstate Highway Act of 1956, which set aside $26 billion to construct 40,000 miles of federal highways, have both a positive and negative impact on America?

1950s Civil Rights Movement

Journal Prompts

- Would the Civil Rights Movement have been as successful as it was if Martin Luther King, Jr. wasn't serving as a pastor at Montgomery's Dexter Avenue Baptist Church in 1955? Explain.

- What do you think most Americans thought in 1957 when they watched on television federal troops escorting the first African-American students to class at Little Rock Central High School while white mobs stood by jeering at the students?

- What role did the principles of civil disobedience play in the 1950s Civil Rights Movement? Would the movement have been as successful as it was if it didn't adhere to these principles? Explain.

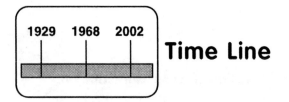

Time Line

Develop a time line listing events relevant to the following themes:
- Rise of Martin Luther King, Jr. as a Civil Rights Leader
- 1950s Civil Rights Movement
- 1950s Civil Rights Legislation and Supreme Court Decisions

Decision-Making Scenarios

- If you were a member of Congress in 1957 when one of the first civil rights bills since Reconstruction was being debated, what would you say when it came your turn to be recognized on the floor of the House?

- If you were a delegate to one of the national political party conventions and found out that TV networks were blotting out podium speeches by African-American delegates so as not to offend Southern stations (which actually occurred), what would you do?

- If you were a young African-American resident of Montgomery, Alabama, in the mid 1950s, would you have joined in the bus boycott? Explain.

1950s Civil Rights Movement *(cont.)*

Concept Maps

Develop a concept map for each of the following:

- Boycott
- Civil Rights
- Desegregation
- "Separate but Equal"

Venn Diagrams

Image of 1950s American Society vs. Reality of 1950s American Society: Compare and contrast the image of the 1950s as a period of economic prosperity, consensus, and conformity with the reality of poverty, segregation, and discrimination.

Post-Civil War Struggle for Civil Rights vs. Post-World War II Struggle for Civil Rights: Compare and contrast the struggle of African Americans for civil rights in the post-Civil War period with that of the post-World War II period.

Vee Heuristics

Brown Decision as an End vs. Brown Decision as a Beginning: How did the unanimous 1954 Supreme Court decision *Brown vs. Board of Education of Topeka, Kansas* mark the end of nearly a century-long struggle while at the same time serve to illustrate the beginning of yet another struggle?

Rosa Parks' Contributions to the Civil Rights Movement vs. Jackie Robinson's Contributions to the Civil Rights Movement: How did the actions and contributions of Rosa Parks and Jackie Robinson to the civil rights movement of the late 1940s and 1950s differ?

Origins of the Vietnam War

Journal Prompts

- Would the war in Vietnam have ever occurred had Presidents Woodrow Wilson or Franklin D. Roosevelt supported Ho Chi Minh's pleas for Indochina's self-determination in the early 20th century?

- How did the stalemate in the Korean War influence American involvement in Vietnam? If there never had been a Korean War would there still have been a war in Vietnam? Explain.

- What is the significance of the fact that the average age of a soldier in the Vietnam War was 19, while the average of a World War II soldier was 26?

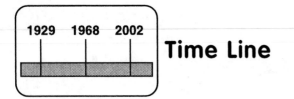

Time Line

Develop a time line listing events relevant to the following themes:

- French Involvement in Vietnam
- American Involvement in Vietnam during Eisenhower Administration
- American Involvement in Vietnam during JFK Administration

Decision-Making Scenarios

- If you were an advisor to President Eisenhower in the 1950s when the French were defeated at Dien Bien Phu and the Geneva Accords of 1954 had just been drafted, what recommendation would you have given the president concerning the proposed 1955 Vietnam elections and further American involvement in Vietnam?

- If you were an advisor to President Kennedy in the early 1960s when the corruption of South Vietnamese President Ngo Dinh Diem was uncovered and an anti-Diem faction was growing in South Vietnam, what recommendation would you have given the president concerning support of the Diem government and further American involvement in Vietnam?

- If you were an advisor to President Johnson in 1968 in the aftermath of the Tet Offensive and in light of the annual cost of the war being $30 billion and 500,000 American troops serving in Southeast Asia, what recommendation would you have given the president concerning further American involvement in Vietnam?

Origins of the Vietnam War *(cont.)*

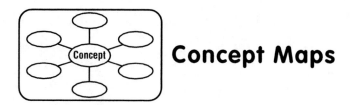

Concept Maps

Develop a concept map for each of the following:

- 17th Parallel
- Domino Theory
- Vietnam Quagmire
- Southeast Asia Treaty Organization (SEATO)

Venn Diagrams

American Involvement in Vietnam under Ike vs. American Involvement in Vietnam under JFK: Compare and contrast the role Presidents Dwight D. Eisenhower and John F. Kennedy played in heightening American involvement in Vietnam.

LBJ's View of Vietnam War vs. Nixon's View of Vietnam War: Compare and contrast Presidents Lyndon B. Johnson and Richard Nixon's view of how best to bring about an end to the war in Vietnam.

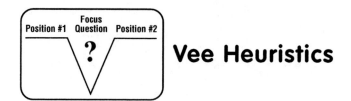

Vee Heuristics

Public Assessment of American Involvement in Vietnam vs. Private Assessment of American Involvement in Vietnam: How did the public and private assessment by U.S. government officials of American involvement in Vietnam during the late 1950s and early 1960s differ?

Vietnam War Causes, Strategies, & Tactics vs. Korean War Causes, Strategies, & Tactics: How did the causes, strategies and tactics of the Vietnam War differ from those of the Korean War?

JFK's New Frontier

Journal Prompts

- Why was the John F. Kennedy White House referred to as a modern-day Camelot? What was the appeal of the Kennedy family to Americans?

- What did President Kennedy mean in his inaugural address when he said, "Ask not what your country can do for you—ask what you can do for your country"? Does this statement still ring true today? Explain.

- How would domestic and foreign policy events during the 1960s have been different had President Kennedy not been assassinated in 1963? Would he be as fondly remembered today? Explain.

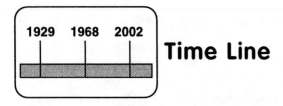

Time Line

Develop a time line listing events relevant to the following themes:

- Political Rise of John F. Kennedy

- Cuban Missile Crisis

- JFK "New Frontier" Economic and Social Initiatives

Decision-Making Scenarios

- If you were an advisor to JFK during the 1960 presidential election campaign, what would you recommend if he asked you what he should do about the Catholic prejudice and anti-Catholic statements some people were making out on the campaign trail?

- If you were one of the "best and brightest" in President Kennedy's cabinet, what advice would you give him if he asked if the United States should invest billions of dollars and perhaps a number of American lives in an effort to land a man on the moon by the end of the decade?

- If you were a student in 1963, what would you do or say when your teacher told your class that fateful day of November 22nd that an assassin had just killed President Kennedy?

JFK's New Frontier *(cont.)*

 ## Concept Maps

Develop a concept map for each of the following:

- Best and Brightest
- Camelot
- "Flexible Response"
- "New Frontier"

 ## Venn Diagrams

JFK's New Frontier Domestic Program vs. JFK's Flexible Response Foreign Policy:
Compare and contrast President John F. Kennedy's domestic program, "New Frontier" objectives, accomplishments, and setbacks with his foreign policy, "Flexible Response" initiatives, accomplishments, and setbacks.

JFK's Role in Bay of Pigs Invasion vs. JFK's Role in Cuban Missile Crisis: Compare and contrast President John F. Kennedy's role in the 1961 Bay of Pigs invasion with the role he played in the 1962 Cuban missile crisis.

 ## Vee Heuristics

JFK's Legacy as a Humanitarian vs. JFK's Legacy as a Cold Warrior: How did President Kennedy's legacy as a humanitarian through his work in support of civil rights and the founding of the Peace Corps differ from his legacy as a Cold Warrior, which resulted from his involvement in Vietnam and CIA plots to assassinate Cuban leader Fidel Castro?

JFK's Presidential Style & Image vs. Ike's Presidential Style & Image: How did John F. Kennedy's presidential style and image differ from that of his predecessor, Dwight D. Eisenhower?

LBJ's Great Society

 ## Journal Prompts

- Was President Lyndon B. Johnson naïve or bold to attempt his War on Poverty? Explain.

- How would American society be different today if LBJ never lobbied to pass such Great Society initiatives as Head Start, Medicare, Job Corps, and the Food Stamps program?

- How would Lyndon B. Johnson be remembered in history had there been no Vietnam War? Is it fair that one decision or event serve to paint the entire historical picture of someone? Explain.

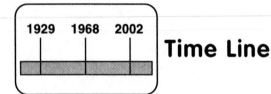 ## Time Line

Develop a time line listing events relevant to the following themes:

- Chief Justice Earl Warren's Court Decisions

- Great Society Programs and Initiatives

- Escalation of the War in Vietnam during the Johnson Administration

 ## Decision-Making Scenarios

- If you were a young African American living in the South during the 1960s, what would you tell President Johnson in a letter after he championed the passing of the Civil Rights Act of 1964 and Voting Rights Act of 1965?

- If you were an advisor to President Johnson and he asked you which Great Society program you would cut and what you would create in its place, what would you tell him and why?

- If you were a member of a poor family in the 1960s that had benefited from President Johnson's War on Poverty programs, what would you tell him if he came to your community while campaigning for a local politician?

LBJ's Great Society *(cont.)*

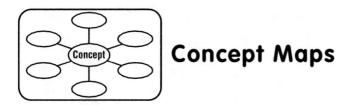

Concept Maps

Develop a concept map for each of the following:

- Great Society
- Gulf of Tonkin Resolution
- The Other America
- "War on Poverty"

Venn Diagrams

LBJ's Great Society vs. FDR's New Deal: Compare and contrast the goals, programs, successes and setbacks of President Lyndon B. Johnson's Great Society with those of his mentor Franklin D. Roosevelt's New Deal.

LBJ's War on Poverty vs. LBJ's War in Vietnam: Compare and contrast President Lyndon B. Johnson's efforts to win his War on Poverty with his efforts to win the war in Vietnam.

Vee Heuristics

President Johnson's Vision for America vs. Senator Goldwater's Vision for America: How did President Johnson's vision for America differ from that of his 1964 presidential election opponent, Republican nominee Senator Barry Goldwater?

LBJ's Civil Rights Record vs. JFK's Civil Rights Record: How did Lyndon B. Johnson's presidential civil rights record differ from that of his fallen predecessor John F. Kennedy?

Vietnam War Protest

Journal Prompts

- What impact, if any, do you think the war protest and peace movement had on bringing about an end to American involvement in Vietnam?

- What impact did television coverage have on public support for American involvement in Vietnam? Would public support have been impacted as much as it was if not for such media coverage? Explain.

- What role did protest songs by such artists as Bob Dylan and Joan Baez play in the anti-war and peace movement of the 1960s?

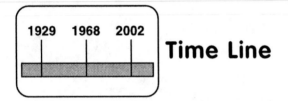

Time Line

Develop a time line listing events relevant to the following themes:

- Escalation of American Involvement in the Vietnam War during the 1960s

- Rise and Fall of Public Support for the Vietnam War

- Emergence of the Vietnam War Protest Movement

Decision-Making Scenarios

- If you were a young college student during the 1960s who witnessed your first anti-war protest, what would you tell your parents about what you saw and heard when you wrote or called home the next time?

- If you were a Democratic member of Congress during the 1960s, would you have broke with your party and Democratic president and called for an end to American involvement in Vietnam, as did Senator J. William Fulbright and others, despite the strong support for such involvement (85% in 1966) in Congress?

- If you were an advisor to President Johnson, what would you tell him to do in response to the student protests on college campuses and elsewhere throughout the United States?

Vietnam War Protest (cont.)

Concept Maps

Develop a concept map for each of the following:

- Doves and Hawks

- "Free Speech Movement"

- Students for a Democratic Society (SDS)

- "Teach-Ins"

Venn Diagrams

Vietnam War Protest & Peace Movement vs. World War I Protest & Peace Movement:
Compare and contrast the Vietnam War protest and peace movement with the protest and peace movement that formed in America during World War I.

Vietnam War Protest Movement Goals, Strategies, & Tactics vs. Civil Rights Movement Goals, Strategies, & Tactics: Compare and contrast the goals, strategies, and tactics of the Vietnam War protest movement with those of the Civil Rights Movement during the 1960s.

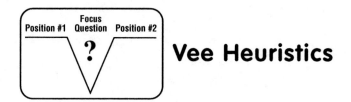

Vee Heuristics

American Military Role in Vietnam in 1960 vs. American Military Role in Vietnam in 1969:
How did America's military role in Vietnam at the beginning of the 1960s differ from that at the end of the decade?

Public Support for Vietnam War in 1960 vs. Public Support for Vietnam War in 1969: How did public support for American involvement in Vietnam at the beginning of the 1960s differ from that at the end of the decade?

1960s: Demand for Equality

Journal Prompts

- Could James Meredith's attendance at the University of Mississippi in 1962—the first African-American student in the history of the university—have been accomplished in any other way than by bringing in 400 federal marshals and 3,000 military troops, at a cost of $4 million? Explain.

- Why was the proposed Equal Rights Amendment, which states that "Equality of rights under the law shall not be denied or abridged by the United States or any state on account of sex," never ratified, despite seven decades of lobbying by women's-rights advocates?

- Were acts like the 1969 occupation of the deserted federal prison at Alcatraz Island in San Francisco Bay the only way that Native-American groups like the American-Indian Movement (AIM) could get the public's attention? Explain.

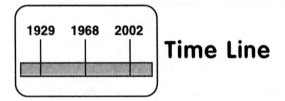

Time Line

Develop a time line listing events relevant to the following themes:

- American Indian Movement
- Feminist Movement
- 1960s Civil Rights Movement

Decision-Making Scenarios

- If you were one of the hundreds of thousands of people who attended Martin Luther King, Jr.'s March on Washington in 1963, what would you write in your diary that night about what you heard and saw that day and about your reaction to King's "I Have a Dream" speech?

- If you were a young person in the 1960s and saw on television news police officers in Birmingham, Alabama, using police dogs, cattle prods, and fire hoses on peaceful civil rights demonstrators, what would you think and do?

- If you were a member of Congress in 1968 when the Bilingual Education Bill, which proposed to reverse state laws that prohibit the teaching of classes in any language other than English, was being debated, what would you say when it came your turn to speak on the floor of the House?

1960s: Demand for Equality *(cont.)*

Concept Maps

Develop a concept map for each of the following:

- American-Indian Movement (AIM)

- Feminism

- Freedom Rides

- United Farm Workers

Venn Diagrams

1960s & '70s Feminist Movement vs. 19th- & Early-20th-Century Women's Rights Movement: Compare and contrast the 1960s and 1970s feminist movement with the Women's Rights movement of the 19th and early 20th century.

Civil Rights Goals & Tactics of Martin Luther King, Jr. vs. Civil Rights Goals & Tactics of Malcolm X: Compare and contrast the goals, tactics, and public image of the two leading African-American civil rights leaders of the 1960s: Martin Luther King, Jr. and Malcolm X.

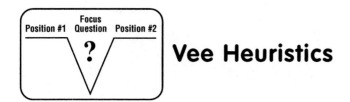

Vee Heuristics

American Indian Movement's Objectives & Tactics vs. Hispanic Leaders' Objectives & Tactics: How did objectives and tactics used by leaders of the American Indian Movement of the 1960s and 1970s differ from those of Hispanic leaders struggling for the same rights?

1960s Civil Rights Movement vs. 1950s Civil Rights Movement: How did the tactics, successes, and setbacks of the 1960s Civil Rights Movement differ from those of the previous decade?

1968: A Turning Point

Journal Prompts

- If the North Vietnamese and Vietcong suffered over 40,000 casualties, 20 percent of their total forces in the Tet Offensive of January 1968, while U.S. and South Vietnamese forces suffered 1,600 casualties, why is this still considered a victory for the North Vietnam military?

- How might the course of American history have been altered had Robert F. Kennedy not been assassinated in 1968?

- What did one U.S. military officer in Vietnam mean by the following statement he made after the destruction of a village in the Mekong delta in 1968: "We had to destroy it in order to save it"?

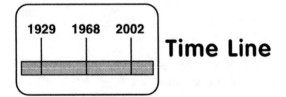

Time Line

Develop a time line listing events relevant to the following themes:

- 1968 Presidential Election Campaigns and Conventions
- Counterculture Movement
- 1968 Events in Vietnam and Paris Peace Talks

Decision-Making Scenarios

- If you were a young person who had worked on the Robert F. Kennedy campaign, how would you feel when you witnessed his assassination on television the night of June 5, 1968?

- If you were a presidential advisor to Lyndon Johnson in April 1968, how would you have tried to prevent the riots that followed the assassination of Martin Luther King, Jr., in Memphis on April 4th, which took place in over 100 cities and resulted in the arrests of 27,000 people?

- If you were a member of the Women's Liberation Movement in 1968, would you have participated in a protest against the Miss America Beauty Pageant that year along with other activists who crowned a sheep as queen?

1968: A Turning Point *(cont.)*

Concept Maps

Develop a concept map for each of the following:

- Counterculture
- Paris Peace Talks
- Tet Offensive
- Women's Lib

Venn Diagrams

MLK Contributions & Legacy vs. RFK Contributions & Legacy: Compare and contrast the contributions and legacy of Martin Luther King, Jr. and Robert F. Kennedy to American society.

1968 Democratic Party Platform vs. 1968 Republican Party Platform: Compare and contrast the domestic and foreign policy positions of the Democratic and Republican Parties in the 1968 presidential election.

Vee Heuristics

Government's Account of Vietnam War vs. Reality of the Tet Offensive: How did the government's account of the war in Vietnam differ from what the nation saw on their televisions in January 1968 during the Tet Offensive?

Conservative View of 1968 Democratic Party Convention vs. Liberal View of 1968 Republican Party Convention: How did more conservative and more liberal-minded Americans view the events at the 1968 Democratic Party Convention in Chicago differently?

Vietnamization & Détente

Journal Prompts

- Was it necessary for President Nixon to "bomb the North Vietnamese delegates back to the negotiations table" at the Paris Peace Talks in 1972? Explain. What is the significance of the fact that only North Vietnam and the United States signed the final peace agreement, while South Vietnam refused?

- Did Richard Nixon and Henry Kissinger achieve "peace with honor" in Vietnam as they proclaimed? Explain.

- How would the United States be different today if the nation didn't become involved in Vietnam, at a cost of 58,000 lives and $150 billion?

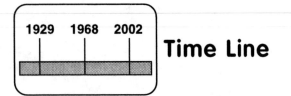

Time Line

Develop a time line listing events relevant to the following themes:

- Vietnamization
- 20th Century US-China Relations
- Détente Treaties and Foreign Policy Initiatives

Decision-Making Scenarios

- If you were a young student at Kent State University or Jackson State University in 1970 and had witnessed the anti-war protests and shootings of some of the student protesters by the military/law enforcement authorities, what would you tell your parents that night when you called home?

- If you were a member of Congress when President Nixon ordered the bombing of Cambodia in an effort to disrupt North Vietnamese supply lines in 1970, without consulting with either the House or Senate, what would you do?

- If you were a magazine reporter sent to cover Richard and Pat Nixon's trip to China in 1972, how would you feel when you arrived in Beijing to the greeting of Foreign Minister Zhou Enlai and the playing of "The Star Spangled Banner"? What would you write in your article about the event?

Vietnamization & Détente *(cont.)*

Concept Maps

Develop a concept map for each of the following:

- Détente
- Nixon Doctrine
- "Ping-Pong Diplomacy"
- Vietnamization

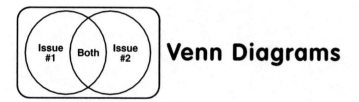

Venn Diagrams

Nixon Doctrine of 1969 vs. Truman Doctrine of 1947: Compare and contrast the causes, objectives, and consequences of the Nixon Doctrine of 1969 with the Truman Doctrine of 1947.

Nixon's Diplomatic & Military Approach in Vietnam War vs. LBJ's Diplomatic & Military Approach in Vietnam War: Compare and contrast the diplomatic and military approaches used by President Richard Nixon in ending the war in Vietnam with those of his predecessor, Lyndon B. Johnson.

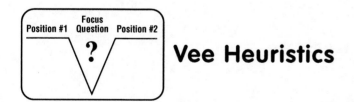

Vee Heuristics

Nixon's 1950s Image & Actions vs. President Nixon's Image & Actions: How did Richard Nixon's image and actions during the 1950s Red Scare and Cold War differ from his image and action as president during the late 1960s and 1970s?

Warren Burger Court vs. Earl Warren Court: How did the ideology and rulings of the Supreme Court under Chief Justice Warren Burger differ from those of his predecessor, Earl Warren?

Watergate & Nixon's Fall

Journal Prompts

- If Richard Nixon was so popular in 1972 that he would go on to win every state in the Union except Massachusetts in the presidential election, why were some members of his campaign staff so nervous or paranoid that they authorized the bugging of the Democratic National Party headquarters?

- Would Richard Nixon have been forced to resign the presidency if he did not practice a policy of tape-recording Oval Office conversations?

- What did a historian mean when he wrote shortly after President Nixon's resignation in August 1974 that this event was "a perfect historical example of 'What goes around, comes around'"? Was he correct?

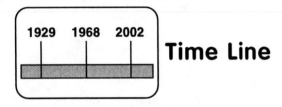

Time Line

Develop a time line listing events relevant to the following themes:

- 1972 Presidential Election
- Watergate Break-In, Trial, and Hearings
- Rise and Fall of Richard Nixon

Decision-Making Scenarios

- If you worked in the Nixon campaign of 1972 and uncovered evidence that the Democratic vice-presidential nominee, Senator Thomas Eagleton, had undergone electric-shock therapy for depression years earlier, would you divulge this information to the press? Explain.

- If you were a young student during the 1970s who watched the Congressional Watergate hearings on television for weeks, how would you respond if your social studies teacher asked you in class what you thought about the whole thing?

- How would you feel if you were Bob Woodward or Carl Bernstein, the *Washington Post* reporters who traced the Watergate break-in back to the Oval Office, and you realized that your investigative reporting would result in the impeachment or resignation of the president of the United States?

Watergate & Nixon's Fall *(cont.)*

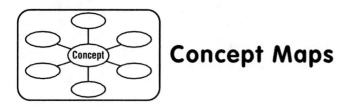

Concept Maps

Develop a concept map for each of the following:

- Committee for the Re-Election of the President (CREEP)
- "Plumbers"
- "Saturday Night Massacre"
- Watergate Tapes

Venn Diagrams

Nixon's Political Successes & Triumphs vs. Nixon's Personal Setbacks & Defeats: Compare and contrast the political successes and triumphs of Richard Nixon with his personal setbacks and defeats.

Positive Legacy of Watergate & Vietnam War vs. Negative Legacy of Watergate & Vietnam War: Compare and contrast the positive and negative legacy of the Watergate scandal and American involvement in the Vietnam War on American society and politics.

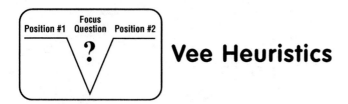

Vee Heuristics

1970s Watergate Scandal vs. 1950s "Checkers Speech" Scandal: How did Richard Nixon's role in the 1970s Watergate scandal differ from the 1950s scandal that resulted in his "Checkers Speech"?

Ford's Pardon of Nixon = Positive vs. Ford's Pardon of Nixon = Negative: What were the positive and negative ramifications of President Gerald Ford's decision to pardon Richard Nixon for his role in the Watergate scandal?

1970s: Ford & Carter Years

Journal Prompts

- How would you feel while you watched the final evacuation of South Vietnam on television in April 29, 1975, with helicopters frantically loading people from atop the U.S. Embassy in Saigon and transporting them to awaiting U.S. naval aircraft carriers moments before the North Vietnamese military seized the former capital of South Vietnam?

- What would you think if you were watching Jimmy Carter's inauguration in 1977 and saw him and his wife walking the trek down Pennsylvania Avenue instead of riding in a limousine?

- Why were Jimmy Carter's televised "fireside chats" in the 1970s not as effective as FDR's radio broadcast "fireside chats" of the 1930s?

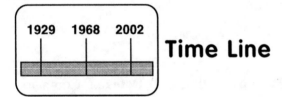

Time Line

Develop a time line listing events relevant to the following themes:

- Nuclear-Arms Talks and Treaties
- Final Chapter in the Vietnam War
- Iranian Hostage Crisis

Decision-Making Scenarios

- If you were an advisor to President Ford, what would you have recommended he do when Cambodian communists seized an unarmed U.S. merchant ship, the *Mayaguez*, and its crew of nearly 40 men?

- If you were President Carter's Secretary of Energy, what would you have recommended be done when OPEC doubled their oil prices in 1979?

- If you were an advisor to President Carter during the Iranian hostage crisis, what would you have suggested the United States do to win the release of those Americans held against their will in Iran?

1970s: Ford & Carter Years *(cont.)*

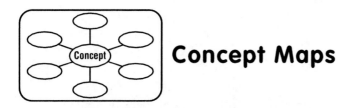

Concept Maps

Develop a concept map for each of the following:

- Bicentennial

- Energy Crisis

- Human Rights

- SALT Talks and Treaties

Venn Diagrams

Gerald Ford's Presidency vs. Jimmy Carter's Presidency: Compare and contrast the presidential leadership style and image, as well as the political setbacks and successes, of Gerald Ford and Jimmy Carter.

America in 1976 vs. America in 1776: Compare and contrast the political, social, and economic status of America in 1976, the year Americans celebrated the bicentennial, with that of 1776, the year that Americans proclaimed their independence.

Vee Heuristics

Carter's 1977 Panama Canal Treaty vs. TR's 1903 Acquisition of the Panama Canal Zone: How did the significance and symbolism of President Jimmy Carter's signing of the Panama Canal Treaty in 1977, which turned over control of the canal to Panamanians in the year 2000, differ from that of President Theodore Roosevelt's acquisition of the rights to the Panama Canal in 1903?

Support for 1980 Olympic Boycott vs. Opposition to 1980 Olympic Boycott: How did Americans differ in their opinion of President Carter's decision to boycott the 1980 Olympic Games to be held in Moscow in protest over the December 1979 Soviet military invasion of Afghanistan?

Reagan Revolution

Journal Prompts

- Why were as many as 60 percent of independent voters and 25 percent of Democrats attracted to Ronald Reagan and his conservative message during the 1980s?

- What was the meaning and significance of the 1984 Ronald Reagan campaign slogan, "Morning in America"? Was this accurate or an exaggeration? Explain.

- How did President Reagan remain so popular even in the midst of the Iran-Contra investigation and hearings of 1987? Why didn't this scandal hurt him in the same way such controversy and scandals impacted other presidents before and after him?

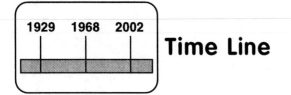

Time Line

Develop a time line listing events relevant to the following themes:

- Resurgence of Conservative Movement in 1980s

- Reaganomics Impact on the American Economy in the 1980s

- 1980s Political Campaigns and Elections

Decision-Making Scenarios

- If you were a voter in the 1980 election, how would you feel about the fact that a former B-grade movie star, who appeared in some films with a chimpanzee named Bonzo, was now running for president? Are there any qualifications, other than those listed in the Constitution, that individuals should meet to run for president? Explain.

- Even though President Reagan reported that he would "never negotiate with terrorists," what would you do if you were a member of the National Security Council and Americans were taken hostage in foreign nations by international terrorists?

- If you were a student during the 1980s and became aware and concerned about the growing national debt, which went from $907 billion in 1980 to $2 trillion in 1986, what would you do?

Reagan Revolution *(cont.)*

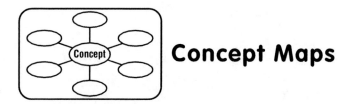

Concept Maps

Develop a concept map for each of the following:

- Affirmative Action
- Moral Majority
- Reaganomics
- Strategic Defense Initiative (SDI), or "Star Wars"

Venn Diagrams

Reagan's Approach to Government & Vision for America vs. Jimmy Carter's Approach to Government & Vision for America: Compare and contrast Ronald Reagan's approach to government and vision for America with that of his predecessor, Jimmy Carter.

1980s Conservative Movement vs. 1950s Conservative Movement: Compare and contrast the conservative shift in American politics and society during the 1980s with that which occurred in the 1950s.

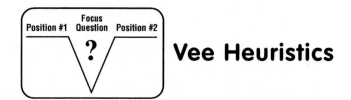

Vee Heuristics

Supply-Side "Reaganomics" Economics vs. Keynesian Economics: How did the principles of supply-side (Reaganomics) economics differ from the more traditional Keynesian economic principles that guided the economic policies of other presidents in the second half of the 20th century?

Reagan's "Best and the Rightest" vs. JFK's "Best and the Brightest": How did the individuals and policies of Ronald Reagan's Cabinet, known as the "best and the rightest," differ from JFK's Cabinet, known as the "best and the brightest"?

End of the Cold War

Journal Prompts

- What did President Reagan mean when he said "we must find peace through strength"? Was he correct? Explain.

- How did President Reagan's reference to the Soviet Union as the "evil empire" differ from the Cold War rhetoric of the 1950s? How was he able to go from this kind of characterization of the Soviets to friendship with Mikhail Gorbachev?

- What did a *Pravda* (the leading Soviet newspaper) editor mean when he said "Gorbachev was unable to change the living standards of the people but he changed the people"? Is this statement accurate? Explain.

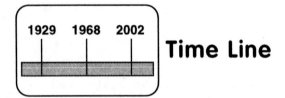

Time Line

Develop a time line listing events relevant to the following themes:

- Rise and Fall of the Berlin Wall

- Period of Gorbachev's *Perestroika* and *Glasnost*

- Foreign Policy Events under Presidents Reagan and Bush

Decision-Making Scenarios

- If you were a newspaper reporter sent to cover the fall of the Berlin Wall in 1989, what would you write in your article so the people back home in the United States might see, hear, and feel what you did at that moment?

- If you were able to interview Ronald Reagan and Mikhail Gorbachev for a student project on the end of the Cold War, what would you ask them?

- If you had an e-mail pal in a former European communist country who said that the end of the Cold War in his or her country hasn't brought the changes everyone thought would happen, at least not as quickly as they thought, what would you tell him or her?

End of the Cold War *(cont.)*

Concept Maps

Develop a concept map for each of the following:

- Contras
- "Evil Empire"
- *Glasnost* and *Perestroika*
- START Talks and Treaties

Venn Diagrams

Individuals & Events Involved in the End of the Cold War vs. Individuals & Events Involved in the Start of the Cold War: Compare and contrast the individuals and events that helped to bring about an end to the Cold War with those individuals and events that played a role in the start of the Cold War nearly a half-century earlier.

Reagan's role in US-USSR Foreign Relations vs. Nixon's Role in US-China Foreign Relations: Compare and contrast the role of Ronald Reagan in reducing the tensions between the United States and Soviet Union during the 1980s with Richard Nixon's role in opening up relations between the United States and China a decade earlier.

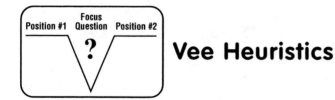

Vee Heuristics

Reagan's Military Buildup vs. Reagan's Arms Reductions Talks: How did the goals and actions of Ronald Reagan in implementing the largest peacetime military buildup in American history differ from those goals and actions taken by the president in the Intermediate Nuclear Forces (INF) Talks and Strategic Arms Reduction Talks (START)?

Bush's Role in Ending the Cold War vs. Reagan's Role in Ending the Cold War: How did George Bush's role in helping to bring an end to the Cold War differ from that of his predecessor, Ronald Reagan?

Gulf War and Bush Presidency

Journal Prompts

- How did the Pentagon's daily briefings during the Gulf War showing bombing attacks with sophisticated military equipment that made the combat missions look more like video games differ from the television images broadcast to everyone's living rooms during the Vietnam War?

- How did the issues surrounding the 1992 Los Angeles riots differ from those of the 1965 Watts riots? How were they the same?

- Would George Bush have won re-election in 1992 if not for H. Ross Perot's decision to throw his hat in the political ring, making it a three-way race? What was Perot's appeal to the American voters in the 1992 contest? Why had this appeal faded by 1996?

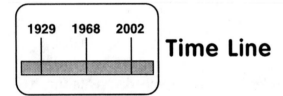

Time Line

Develop a time line listing events relevant to the following themes:

- Gulf War: Battlefield
- Gulf War: Home Front
- George Bush Domestic and Foreign Policy

Decision-Making Scenarios

- If you were an advisor to President Bush at the 1992 Earth Summit in Brazil, what would you recommend if he asked for your advice on the proposed resolution that would pledge the nation's support for biodiversity?

- If you were a reporter sent to cover the *Exxon Valdez* oil tanker spill in Alaska, what would you write in your article about the significance of this event?

- How would you feel if you were studying the American Revolution in your social studies class, only to go home that night to see the 1989 pro-democracy demonstrations at Tianamen Square in Beijing, China, which included the parading of a homemade Statue of Liberty?

Gulf War and Bush Presidency (cont.)

Concept Maps

Develop a concept map for each of the following:

- *Exxon Valdez*
- Gulf War
- Los Angeles Riots
- Tiananmen Square

Venn Diagrams

President Bush Foreign Policy Accomplishments & Setbacks vs. President Bush Domestic Policy Accomplishments & Setbacks: Compare and contrast the foreign policy and domestic policy accomplishments and setbacks experienced by President George Bush.

American Involvement in the Gulf War vs. American Involvement in the Vietnam War: Compare and contrast American involvement in the Gulf War with that of the next most recent war in American history, the Vietnam War.

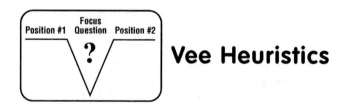

Vee Heuristics

Pro-Democracy Movement in China vs. Pro-Democracy Movement in Europe: How did events and results of the pro-democracy movement in China during the late 20th century differ from those of the pro-democracy movement in Europe during this same period?

America's Relationship with Dictators During the Cold War vs. America's Relationship with Dictators in the Post-Cold War Period: How did America's relationship with military dictators in Central and South America (e.g., Augusto Pinochet in Chile, Manuel Noriega in Panama) in the Cold War era differ from that in the post-Cold War period?

The Clinton Years: Economic Boom and Political Scandal

Journal Prompts

- Were Bill Clinton's two terms in office evidence that his 1992 campaign claim, "It's the economy, stupid," was indeed true? Besides economics, what other issues were of major concern to American voters?

- Did Hillary Rodham Clinton's duties and accomplishments as first lady illustrate the changing role of the first lady, or did they provide yet another example of the consistency in the type of individuals who have occupied that position (from Abigail Adams to Eleanor Roosevelt to Hillary Clinton)?

- Why was Bill Clinton known as the "comeback kid"? Is this an accurate characterization of the former president? Explain.

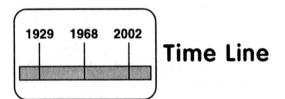

Time Line

Develop a time line listing events relevant to the following themes:

- 1990s Political Campaigns and Elections
- 1990s Social Tensions and Violence
- Investigation and Impeachment of President Clinton

Decision-Making Scenarios

- If you were a campaign advisor for Bill Clinton in 1992, what would you recommend if he asked you if he should appear on MTV and other television talk shows? What if he asked you what you thought he should say if asked to play the saxophone? Explain.

- If you were appointed to a campaign-finance-reform task force following the 1996 presidential election, in which over $650 million was spent on the two major campaigns, what would be your recommendation?

- If you were a member of the U.S. House of Representatives in 1998, would you have voted to impeach President Clinton? Explain why or why not.

The Clinton Years: Economic Boom and Political Scandal *(cont.)*

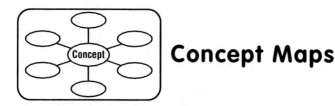

Concept Maps

Develop a concept map for each of the following:

- "It's the Economy, Stupid"
- North American Free Trade Agreement (NAFTA)
- Oklahoma City Bombing
- Whitewater

Venn Diagrams

Clinton's Presidential Leadership Style & Political Vision vs. Reagan and Bush's Presidential Leadership Style & Political Vision: Compare and contrast Bill Clinton's presidential leadership style and political vision for America with that of his two Republican predecessors, Ronald Reagan and George Bush.

Impeachment Trial of Bill Clinton vs. Impeachment Trial of Andrew Johnson: Compare and contrast the issues and events involved in the 1999 impeachment trial of President Bill Clinton with those of the 1868 impeachment trial of President Andrew Johnson.

Vee Heuristics

Late 20th Century Political Scandals vs. Gilded Age Political Scandals: How did the political scandals of the late 20th century differ from those of the Gilded Age?

Clinton-Era Economic Boom vs. Reagan-Era Economic Boom: How did the causes and consequences of the Clinton-era economic boom differ from those of the Reagan-era boom?

A New Millennium

Journal Prompts

- During the first half of the 20th century, the automobile had perhaps the greatest impact of any item on the American landscape; what item do you believe will replace the automobile in that position during the first half of the 21st century? Explain.

- Why did members of the George W. Bush Administration state that the War on Terrorism would be like the Cold War? Is this an appropriate comparison? Explain.

- Compare and contrast the treatment of Arab-Americans during the War on Terrorism with that of Japanese-Americans during World War II.

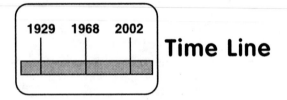

Time Line

Develop a time line listing events relevant to the following themes:

- Emergence of the Information Society

- Incidents of Terrorism Against the United States

- War on Terrorism

Decision-Making Scenarios

- If you were a young entrepreneur during the late 20th and early 21st century, what "dot-com" company would you start up? Explain why.

- If you were a journalist sent to cover the attack on the World Trade Center and the rescue operation that followed, what would you write in your article?

- If you were appointed to serve in the newly created Office of Homeland Security, what would you recommend be done to combat terrorism in the United States?

A New Millennium *(cont.)*

 ## Concept Maps

Develop a concept map for the following:

- Digital Divide

- Internet

- Terrorism

- September 11, 2001

 ## Venn Diagrams

2000 Presidential Election Controversy & Resolution vs. 1876 Presidential Election Controversy & Resolution: Compare and contrast the controversy surrounding the 2000 presidential election, and the manner in which it was resolved, with the controversy and resolution of the 1876 presidential contest.

Goals, Tactics, and Strategies Used to Fight War on Terrorism vs. Goals, Tactics, and Strategies Used to Fight Conventional Wars: Compare and contrast the goals, tactics, and strategies used by the United States to fight the War on Terrorism with those used to fight conventional 20ᵗʰ-century wars, such as World War II.

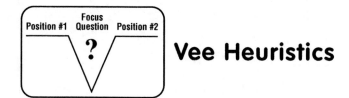 ## Vee Heuristics

Causes, Events, and Response to December 7, 1941 vs. Causes, Events, and Response to September 11, 2001: How did the causes, events, and response to the attack on Pearl Harbor on December 7, 1941, differ from those involving the attacks on the World Trade Center and the Pentagon on September 11, 2001?

Promises and Problems in the New Millennium vs. Promises and Problems in 1900: How do the promises and problems that America faces at the dawn of the new millennium differ from those the nation faced in 1900?

Journal Prompt

Template

Journal Prompt *(cont.)*

Templates

Journal Prompt #1

Journal Prompt #2

Journal Prompt #3

Time Line

Template

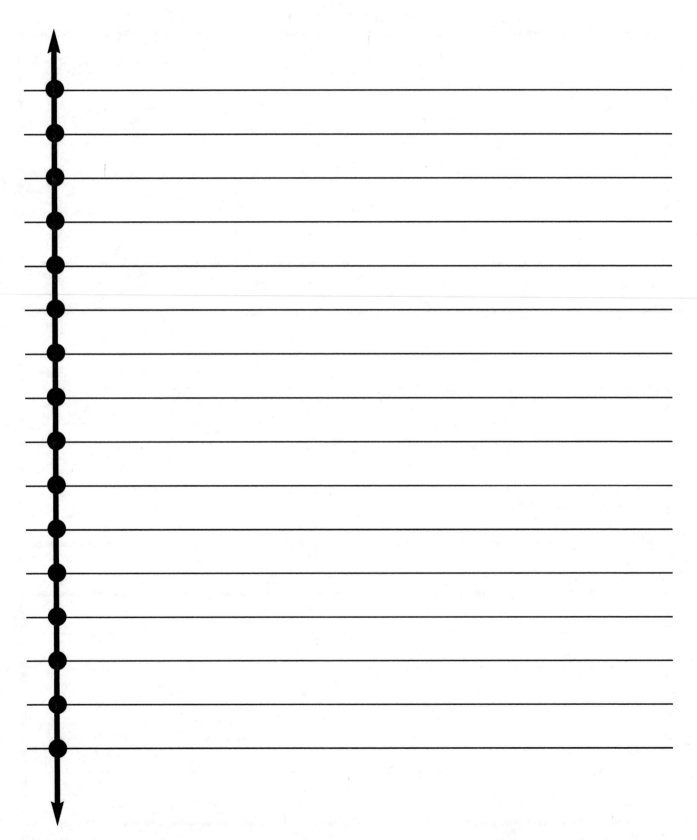

Time Line *(cont.)*

Templates

Time Line #1

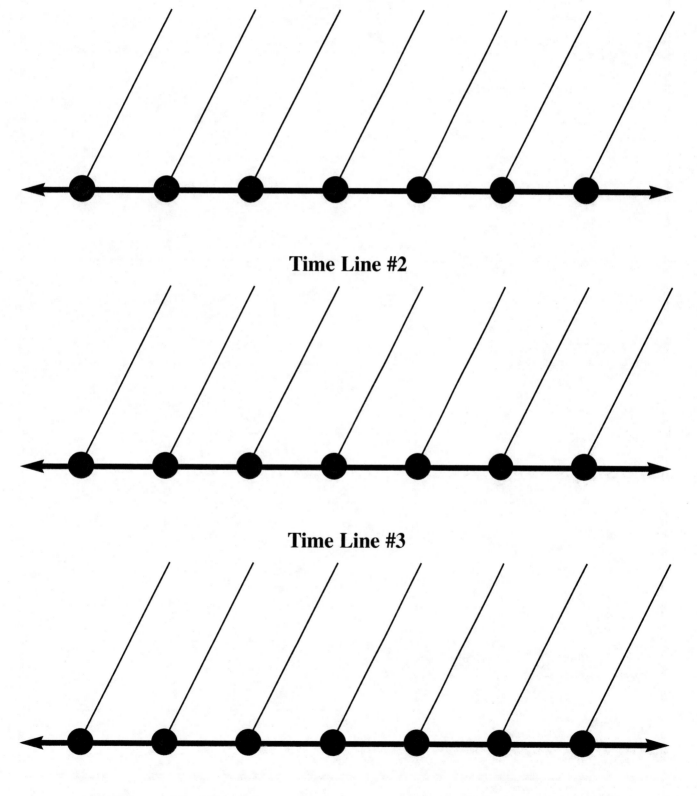

Time Line #2

Time Line #3

Decision-Making Scenario

Template

Decision-Making Scenario *(cont.)*

Template

Decision-Making Scenario #1

Decision-Making Scenario #2

Decision-Making Scenario #3

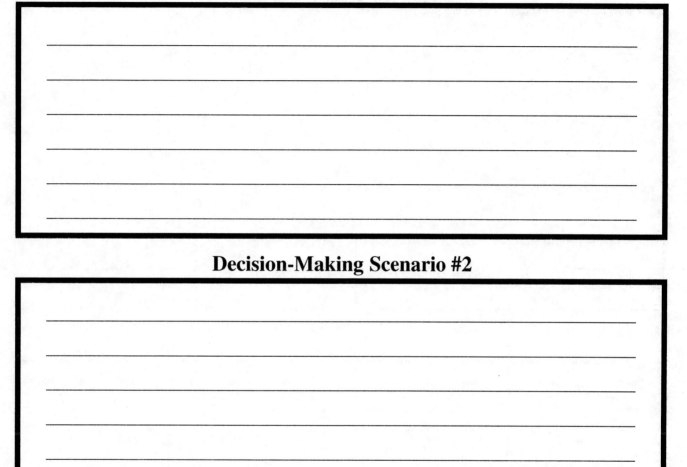

Decision-Making Scenario (Chart Format)

Template

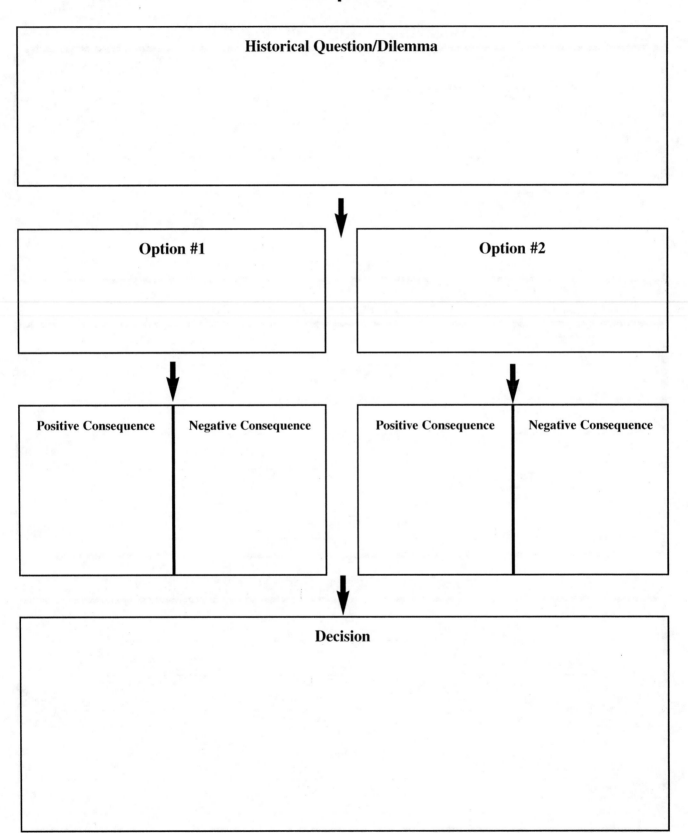

Historical Question/Dilemma

Option #1

Option #2

Positive Consequence	Negative Consequence

Positive Consequence	Negative Consequence

Decision

Concept Map

Template

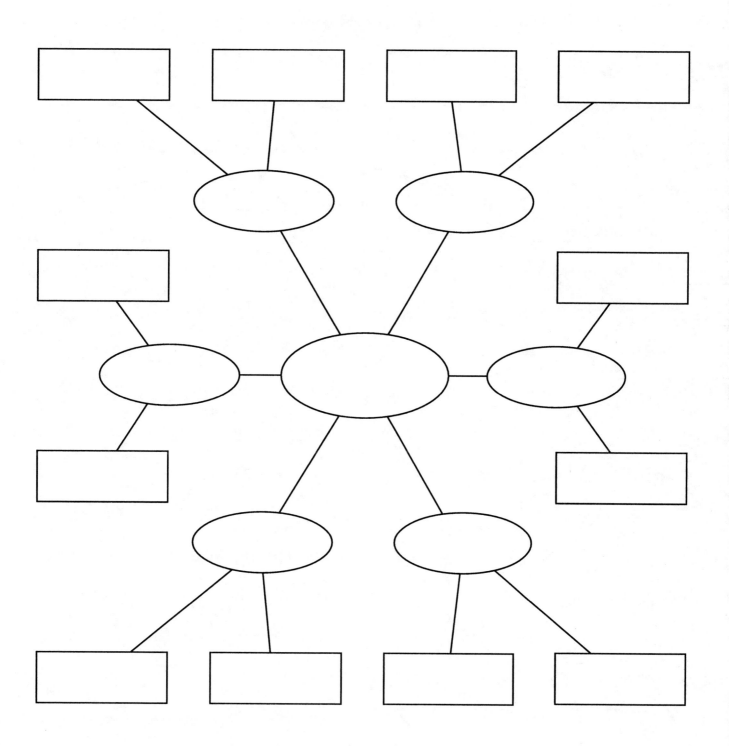

Concept Map *(cont.)*

Templates

Concept Map #1

Concept Map #2

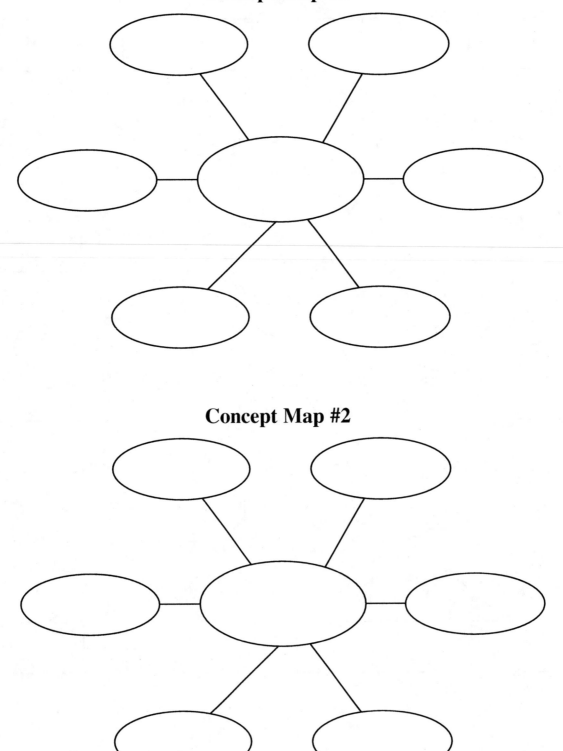

Concept Map *(cont.)*

Templates

Concept Map #3

Concept Map #4

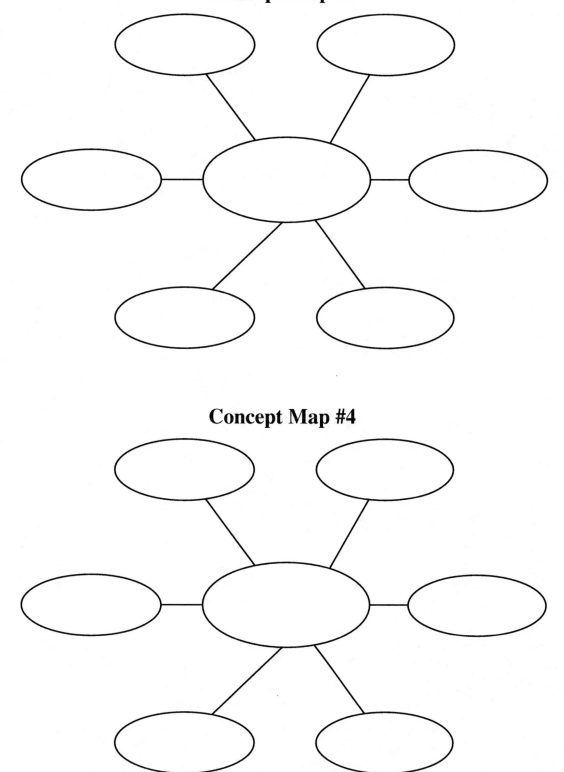

Venn Diagram

Template

1. _____   2. _____

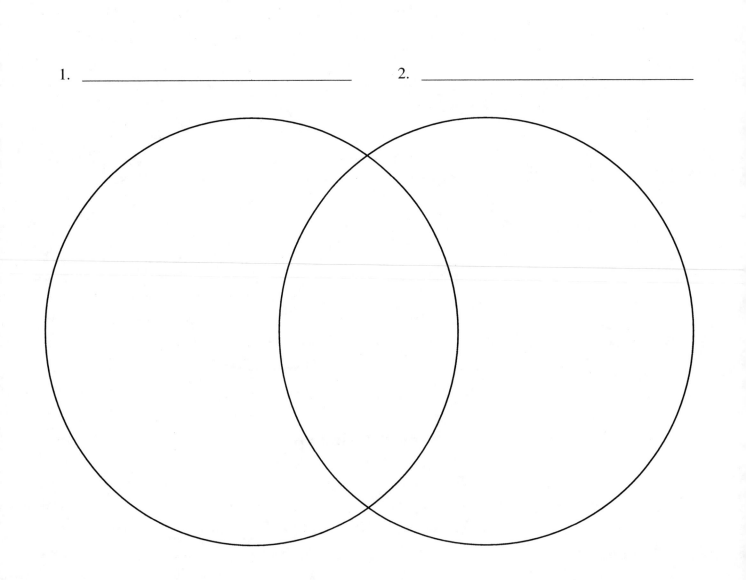

Venn Diagram *(cont.)*

Templates

Venn Diagram #1

1. _____   1. _____

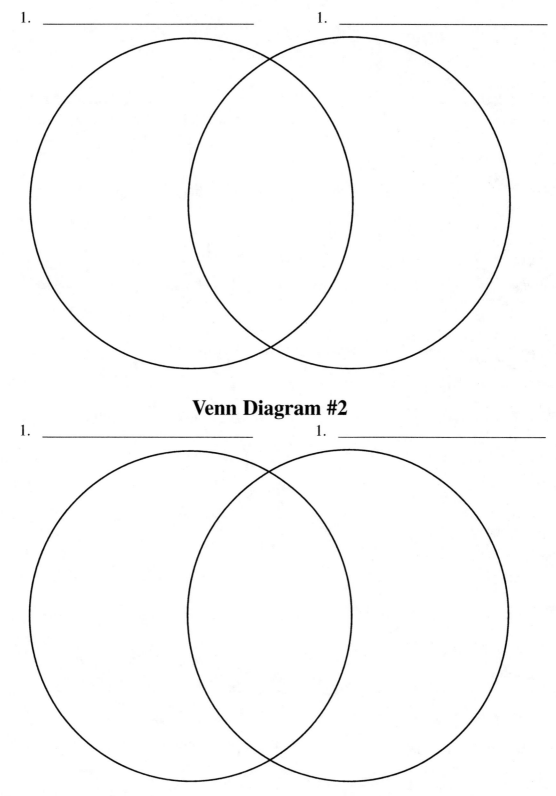

Venn Diagram #2

1. _____   1. _____

Vee Heuristic

Template

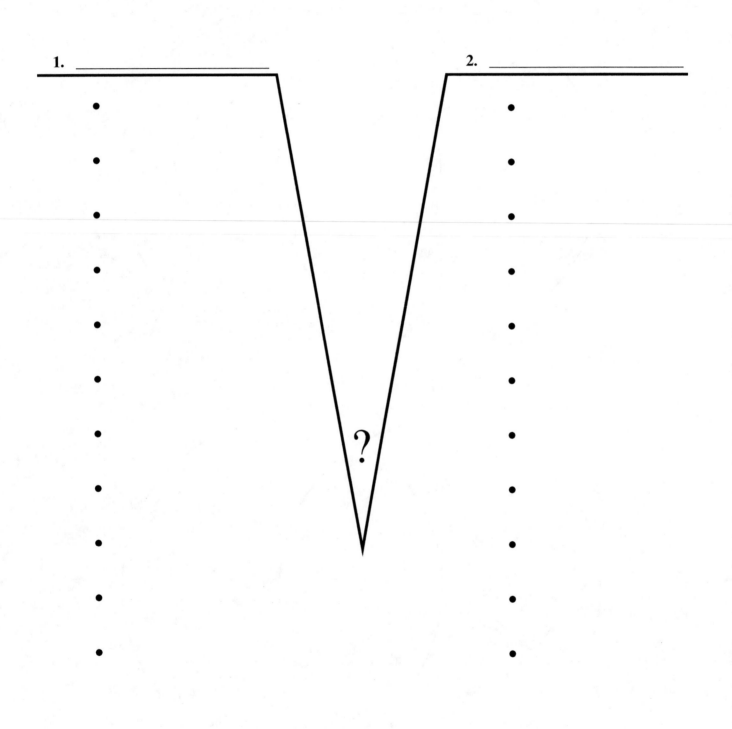

1. _____

2. _____

?

Vee Heuristic *(cont.)*

Templates

Vee Heuristic #1

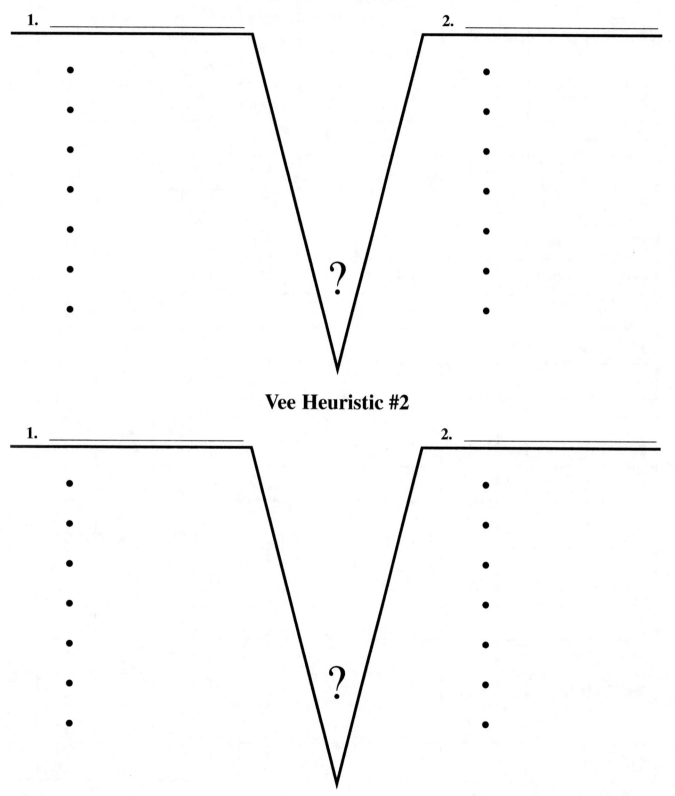

Vee Heuristic #2

Activities Checklist

Activity	Theme Number																	
	1	2	3	4	5	6	7	8	9	10	11	12	13	14	15	16	17	18
Journal																		
#1																		
#2																		
#3																		
Time Line																		
#1																		
#2																		
#3																		
Decision-Making																		
#1																		
#2																		
#3																		
Concept Map																		
#1																		
#2																		
#3																		
#4																		
Venn Diagram																		
#1																		
#2																		
Vee Heuristic																		
#1																		
#2																		

Activities Checklist *(cont.)*

Activity	Theme Number																	
	19	20	21	22	23	24	25	26	27	28	29	30	31	32	33	34	35	36
Journal																		
#1																		
#2																		
#3																		
Time Line																		
#1																		
#2																		
#3																		
Decision-Making																		
#1																		
#2																		
#3																		
Concept Map																		
#1																		
#2																		
#3																		
#4																		
Venn Diagram																		
#1																		
#2																		
Vee Heuristic																		
#1																		
#2																		

Activities Checklist *(cont.)*

Activity	Theme Number																	
	37	38	39	40	41	42	43	44	45	46	47	48	49	50	51	52	53	54
Journal																		
#1																		
#2																		
#3																		
Time Line																		
#1																		
#2																		
#3																		
Decision-Making																		
#1																		
#2																		
#3																		
Concept Map																		
#1																		
#2																		
#3																		
#4																		
Venn Diagram																		
#1																		
#2																		
Vee Heuristic																		
#1																		
#2																		

Activities Checklist *(cont.)*

Activity	Theme Number																	
	55	56	57	58	59	60	61	62	63	64	65	66	67	68	69	70	71	72
Journal																		
#1																		
#2																		
#3																		
Time Line																		
#1																		
#2																		
#3																		
Decision-Making																		
#1																		
#2																		
#3																		
Concept Map																		
#1																		
#2																		
#3																		
#4																		
Venn Diagram																		
#1																		
#2																		
Vee Heuristic																		
#1																		
#2																		

Resources

Books

Andrade, Albert and Shari Tishman. *Critical Squares: Games of Critical Thinking and Understanding.* Teacher Ideas Press, 1997.

Cantu, D. Antonio. *Presidential Elections: 1789-1996.* Discovery Enterprises, Ltd., 1998.

Carey, John. *Eyewitness to History.* Avon Books, 1990.

Crabtree, Charlotte, Gary B. Nash, Paul Gagnon, and Scott Waugh. *Lessons from History: Essential Understandings and Historical Perspectives Students Should Acquire.* National Center of History in the Schools, 1992.

Davis, Kenneth C. *Don't Know Much About History: Everything You Need to Know About American History But Never Learned.* Crown Publishers, Inc., 1990.

Furay, Conal and Michale J. Salevouris. *The Methods and Skills of History: A Practical Guide.* Harlan Davidson, Inc., 1988.

Gonick, Larry. *The Cartoon History of the United States.* HarperPerennial, 1991.

Holt, Patricia Lee. *George Washington Had No Middle Name: Strange Historical Facts from the Days of the Greeks and Romans up to the Present.* Citadel Press, 1998.

Jorgensen, Karen L. *History Workshop: Reconstructing the Past with Elementary Students.* Heinmann, 1993.

King, David C. *First Facts about American Heroes.* Scholastic, Inc., 1996.

Lockwood, Alan L. and David E. Harris. *Reasoning with Democratic Values: Ethical Problems in United States History (Vols. I & II).* Teachers College Press, 1985.

Percoco, James A. *A Passion for the Past: Creative Teaching of U.S. History.* Heinmann, 1998.

Shenkman, Richard. *I Love Paul Revere, Whether He Rode or Not.* HarperPerennial, 1992.

Shenkman, Richard. *Legends, Lies & Cherished Myths of American History.* Perennial Library, 1989.

Shenkman, Richard and Kurt Reiger. *One-Night Stands with American History: Odd, Amusing, and Little-Known Incidents.* Quill, 1982.

Whitcomb, John and Claire Whitcomb. *Oh Say Can You See: Unexpected Anecdotes About American History.* Quill, 1987.

Web Sites

African-American Odyssey: http://lcweb2.loc.gov/ammem/aaohtml/exhibit/aointro.html

Atlas of U.S. Presidential Elections: http://uselectinoatlas.org

C-Span American Presidents Life Portraits: http://www.americanpresidents.org

Historical Maps of the United States: http://www.lib.utexas.edu/maps/histus/html

Library of Congress (LOC) American Memory History Collection: http://memory.loc.gov/ammem/amhome.html

National Archives and Records Administration (NARA) Picturing the Century Exhibit: http://www.nara.gov/exhall/picturing_the_century/galleries/galleries.html

NARA Digital Classroom: http://www.nara.gov/education

NARA Research Room: http://www.nara.gov/research/

PBS History Neighborhood: http://www.pbs.org/neighborhoods/history/

Portraits of the Presidents and First Ladies: http://memory.loc.gov/ammem/odmdhtml/preshome.html

POTUS Presidents of the United States: http://www.ipl.org/ref/POTUS/

Presidential Inaugurations: http://memory.loc.gov/ammem/pihtml/pimenu.html

White House History of Presidents of the United States: http://www.whitehouse.gov/history/presidents/

Yale Avalon Project Collection of Historical Documents: http://www/yale.edu/lawweb/avalon/avalon.htm